MW01097368

DAD,
CAN I BORROW
THE HEARSE?

The views and opinions expressed in this book are solely those of the author and do not reflect the views or opinions of Gatekeeper Press. Gatekeeper Press is not to be held responsible for and expressly disclaims responsibility of the content herein.

DAD, CAN I BORROW THE HEARSE?

Published by Gatekeeper Press
2167 Stringtown Rd, Suite 109
Columbus, OH 43123-2989
www.GatekeeperPress.com

Copyright © 2021 by Thomas J. Van Kula
All rights reserved. Neither this book, nor any parts within it may be sold or reproduced in any form or by any electronic or mechanical means, including information storage and retrieval systems, without permission in writing from the author. The only exception is by a reviewer, who may quote short excerpts in a review.

The cover design, interior formatting, typesetting, and editorial work for this book are entirely the product of the author. Gatekeeper Press did not participate in and is not responsible for any aspect of these elements.

ISBN (hardcover): 9781662913808
eISBN: 9781662913815

DAD,
CAN I BORROW
THE HEARSE?

Thomas J. Van Kula

gatekeeper press

Columbus, Ohio

THIS BOOK IS DEDICATED
TO MY FATHER,
GEORGE VAN KULA.

Complete
Funeral Service
*Reasonable
Prices*

GEORGE
VAN KULA

Geo. Van Kula Funeral Home
MODERN CHAPEL - LICENSED EMBALMER
9074 ST. CYRIL, corner MARCUS ....PLAZA 437C

"Dad, Can I Borrow The Hearse?"

"Life Stories, Life Stories. Everyone's Doing Life
Stories. Why Don't They Do My Life Story? I Might Have Lived."
Henny Youngman

"Life Is Worth Living"
Bishop Fulton J. Sheen

"You Can Lead A Horse To Water, But A Pencil Must Be Lead"
Soupy Sales

"If You Don't Go To Somebody's Funeral, They Won't Come To Yours"
Yogi Berra

PREFACE

I put on a performance no one wanted to attend – a funeral. I was a symbol of something no one wanted to be reminded of – Death. I was a Funeral Director.

My first visit to a funeral home transpired on March 7, 1943 – I was five days old. We resided upstairs. Over the duration of the next four decades I lived with death on a daily basis.

Almost everyone at some point in their life has crossed paths with a member of the Funeral Director fraternity. Whether these encounters were of a professional or social nature I'm confident that in the majority of situations the Funeral Director projected a positive public image. Unfortunately on the other hand there still remains today the stereotyped "Hollywood Portrayal" of those in funeral service as stoic, humorless, bungling buffoons. In my opinion this description is more fitting of Hollywood.

Reflecting on my own personal interaction throughout the years I can verify that the majority of Funeral Directors are dedicated professionals of the highest ethical and moral character. As in any other profession there are those who fall beneath the radar and funeral service is no exception but their ranks are minimal.

As an observer and eventual practitioner of one the world's oldest professions, I have borne witness to human nature under the most demanding of emotional circumstances. In the following pages of rhetoric I have attempted to present a summary of events as they related to me – "The Funeral Director's Kid".

CONTENTS

Chapter One   Before Their Time   1

Chapter Two   Slovakia To The Promised Land   9

Chapter Three   Pennsylvania To The Motor City   15

Chapter Four   The Beginning   21

Chapter Five   The "1940'S"   31

Chapter Six   World War II   59

Chapter Seven   The "1950'S"   67

Chapter Eight   The "1960'S"   117

Chapter Nine   The "1970'S"   145

Chapter Ten   Fast Forward   193

CHAPTER ONE

"BEFORE THEIR TIME"

One of the more consequential facts of life that I absorbed early on was that death placed no restrictions on age. The death of a child is one of the greatest tragedies of parenthood. In my own humble opinion nothing on the face of the earth can compare to the grief experience involved in that dastardly act of fate. For the initial four and a half decades of my existence I was associated with the process of burying the dead. When families called to avail themselves of our services we were perceived to be pillars of strength for them to lean on. At times the difficulty of this task stretched mental endurance to its limits.

The act of burying children was foreign to my senses. As a youngster growing up in a funeral home environment I found it difficult to perceive. No school or curriculum, Mortuary Science or other, no amount of experience, no amount of religious rhetoric and upbringing can adequately prepare you for the emotional roller coaster you experience in burying a child. Old people died – you expected that – it's a fact of life. Children and babies didn't die – it wasn't fair – they never had a chance at life. But they did die: They were born dead, they died of SIDS (crib death), they died of leukemia, they were run over and crushed by cars, trucks, motorcycles, they drowned, they suffered a tragic death by fire and to me the most heinous atrocity known to mankind – they were

1

murdered. Babies, infants, toddlers, children, teenagers – I buried them all.

Poignant emotions currently flood my thought process as I reflect back on the funerals of children and young adults that I was involved with throughout my career in funeral service. One afternoon I noticed my Dad exiting the house with a small black valise. My young inquisitive mind questioned his destination – was he going out of town? He explained in fatherly tones that a baby was born dead and he was going to the hospital to make the removal. At the age of 16 with the acquisition of my driver's license I inherited the black valise. With few exceptions in the ensuing quarter century I became the official stillborn conveyor.

Upon presentation of the official paperwork to the appropriate hospital personnel you were escorted to the morgue. After careful and thorough examination of the attached ID I carefully placed the baby into the blanket lined carrying case. As I traversed the maze of hospital corridors to the relevant exit I often wondered if anyone was aware of my mission. How many times have we witnessed the hospital scene involving the mother and newborn surrounded by the smiling staff and grandparents as they exited the hospital with the proud father behind the wheel of the family vehicle for the trip home? Then there I was alone in the subterranean bowels and passageways of the hospital basement transporting a lifeless newborn to an awaiting vehicle for an impending journey to the cemetery.

Whether viewing was scheduled or not clothing for the infant was generally brought in by the father or grandparents. Usually accompanying the apparel was a rattle or stuffed animal more often than not from a brother or sister. Outfitting the remains and placing them in the casket became one of my assigned tasks – it was an emotional experience. Trying to rationalize the situation I kept reminding myself that this tiny lifeless baby was currently in a far better place than I was. Viewing of the remains and the observance of a religious service at the cemetery were options reserved for the parents. Although stillborn deaths affected me I could accept them with some sort of rationality. They were born dead and although a sad commentary in itself, they never experienced that breath of life, their cries were never heard by moms or dads, brothers and sisters, their smiles and cooing were silenced before they had a chance to be seen or heard.

Whether the time span involved were hours, days, months or years I experienced more difficult moments in accepting the death of children that lived. Nestled among the multitude of storage containers lining the shelves of the funeral home basement storage area was a complete layout ensemble for children's funerals. The first time I recollect it being put to use was for the brother of a childhood friend – a victim of leukemia. Although he was six years younger than myself he was a member of a fairly close neighborhood fraternity of kids and his death affected us all.

As I progressed through my hearse and limousine driving excursions, resident training and eventual licensure I became more immersed in the tragedy of childhood death. Five identical black Cadillac hearses preceded an armada of vehicles through suburban thoroughfares as the funeral cortege maneuvered from funeral home, to church and cemetery. Six caskets containing the remains of a family occupied the five hearses – victims of an airplane crash. The fifth hearse containing the two white caskets of the youngest family members was driven by me.

Returning from a service on a typical Michigan summer day of oppressive heat and humidity Dad and I were unwinding in the air conditioned comfort of the Sterling Heights office when the moment was interrupted with the ringing of the phone. Upon answering I was greeted by the voice of a young female who informed me she was calling on behalf of her deaf parents. She informed me that her four year old sister had drowned in a neighbor's swimming pool and they wanted to come in and make arrangements. Initial thoughts suggested that this might be a crank call – perhaps it was the maturity and sincerity of her manner of speaking that convinced me to dismiss the prank theory almost immediately – I believed her. Within the hour the 11 year old entered the funeral home accompanied by her parents and aunt. The young lady was mature beyond her years as she assisted her parents in planning the funeral of her little sister. It was a tragedy for a family that was already dealt a less than ideal hand in life.

Holding my emotions in check was most difficult when I had the obligation of escorting parents for the first time to the casket containing their child. I had to suppress any thoughts or actions that would add to an already emotional moment. My feelings and heart went out to those parents and family members and I shared in their grief and sorrow. On more than one occasion I stepped away to dry a tear from my eye.

Entering my darkened hotel room my attention was immediately focused on the blinking red light on the phone signaling a message. Dialing home I instinctively surmised that my attendance at the Chicago Rotary convention would be terminated with the placement of the call – it was. A 13 year old girl was savagely murdered in her residence within a mile of the Sterling Heights funeral home. Returning home from her classes at the local junior high she surprised an intruder and was brutally attacked with a hammer. As my flight back sped across the Michigan skies I attempted to question the degree of civility present in today's society. What type of person would attack a defenseless young girl in the safety of her

4

home and end her life, her hopes, her dreams, her future? Not to mention the grief and sorrow that traumatized her family. I wish it would have been possible for every liberal bleeding heart opponent of the death penalty to have been present when I first witnessed this poor child's lifeless remains. A civilized society – I think we have a way to go. But what can we expect when politicians place a greater emphasis on their quest for re-election and inflating their egotistical self-importance than providing adequate funding and resources for mental health.

I greeted them at the front door of the Sterling Heights funeral home – a young married couple not unlike myself and a cadre of my friends. Following the rendering of formal introductions we proceeded to the arrangements office. With heavy hearts they informed me that their two year old son was hospitalized and in the final stages of his young life – they were present to make arrangements for his funeral. My emotional psyche was about to be put to the test once again. I would attempt with every ounce of God given ability to make things as comfortable as humanly possible in this their time of grief and sorrow, their hell on earth and this moment that parents everywhere pray to God never befalls them. A few days following their initial visit I was awakened at 2 AM by a phone call - on the line was a family member informing me that the child had died - contacting my neighbor and colleague Ed Jeszke we drove to the family home. Lights were on in almost every room as we approached the residence betraying the hour of the night. The child's Dad met us at the front door where I expressed my condolences as the grieving father ushered us inside. Seated in a rocking chair was the young mother gently rocking her dead son – they had brought him home to die. In what I would construe to be one of the most heartrending moments in my career in funeral service I reached down and gently removed her son from her maternal grasp. Upon completing the transfer of the body to the funeral home and delivering Ed to his I returned to mine. As I wearily reached the top of the stairway I entered the bedroom on the right glanced down and gave my two year old son a tear filled kiss goodnight.

Heavy-hearted memories remain – The teddy bears and baby rattles in the miniature caskets, pictures of brothers and sisters placed in small lifeless hands, a sibling crayon drawing pinned to the white lined casket lid, parents, grandparents and friends consoling each other with wordless tear-filled hugs of affection, the letter sweater and hockey stick being placed in the 16 year olds' casket by an inconsolable Dad, my carrying the casket from the limousine to the grave bearing an 18 month old SIDS victim – the daughter of family friends, the guiding of the ten year olds' casket down the middle aisle of the church and focusing my tear filled eyes straight ahead and avoiding the tear filled eyes of his classmates in the pews of the overflowing church scene.

All of the above – vital statistics legally registered with the Department of Health of the State of Michigan and now only poignant memories of their respective families and me – the funeral directors' kid.

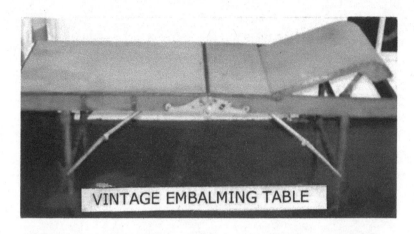
VINTAGE EMBALMING TABLE

"THE BLACK VALISE"

VINTAGE EMBALMING MACHINE
CIRCA 1930'S

CHAPTER TWO

SLOVAKIA TO THE PROMISED LAND

Slovakia or the Slovak Republic is a landlocked country in Central Europe bordered by Austria to the west, The Czech Republic to the Northwest, Hungary to the South, Poland to the North and The Ukraine to the East. Slovakia's mountainous territory spans over 19,000 square miles. From the 11th century until 1918 it was under the control of the Austrian-Hungarian Empire. In 1918 it became known as Czecho-Slovakia, an alliance forced upon them by the major powers after World War 1 and the subsequent dismantling of the Austrian-Hungarian Empire.

Ostrov is a village in the Sobrance District in the Kosice Region of Eastern Slovakia, approximately 10 miles from the Ukranian border. It was here in March of 1861 that my paternal grandfather, George Van Kula was penned in as the newest member on the village rolls.

Widowed with two infant daughters, he remarried in the spring of 1895. Not anticipating much of a future in peasantry, he set out for "America" – "The Promised Land". At this point in time immigration to America was beginning to establish a foothold in the villages throughout Central Europe.

9

Following the Civil War the USA was experiencing an industrial revolution and one commodity that was in short supply was "cheap labor". The industrialists discovered it in the villages of Slovakia, Bohemia, Poland, Italy and throughout Europe. Coal and steel companies contracted with steamship operators, who in turn hired agents to traverse the highways and byways of the European countryside to promote and extol the virtues of the "Original 48". They hired workers and sold steamship tickets - an additional incentive for the villagers were the letters from relatives and friends who had previously immigrated to the USA inviting them to join them and work for those American "Greenbacks".

Travelling overland 800 miles from Ostrov, Slovakia to Bremen, Germany Grandpa George set sail on the liner "Stuttgart" and arrived at Ellis Island on April 10, 1895. Family historical records on the journey have been lost in time, but an educated guess is that he might have travelled with a fellow villager or had a contact in Pennsylvania. After successfully passing through the bureaucratic maze of Ellis Island he ventured to Gallitzin, Pennsylvania worked the mines and eventually settled in Continental #2, South Union Township, Fayette County, Pennsylvania.

My grandfather's excursion was a "Most Remarkable Journey". He held the Van Kula "Most Remarkable Journey" title for approximately one year. In 1896 my grandmother, Anna (Janus) Van Kula duplicated it and surpassed it in terms of remarkable – she did it with two toddlers, ages 2 and 4. Sitting here 125 years after the fact I find it very difficult to comprehend how this petite lady accomplished this feat: A 4800 mile journey across two continents, crossing the Atlantic in less than ideal accommodations, limited English (if any at all), meager finances and attending to the needs and fears of two young girls. Their journey terminated at Continental #2, located at the base of Chestnut Ridge – the westernmost ridge of the Appalachian Mountains to the east in Southwestern Pennsylvania.

Details concerning their transatlantic ventures are at a minimum. It would have been a blessing to have at our disposal the anecdotal facts and recollections of these two remarkable journeys. It would have been a greater blessing if I would have had the opportunity to spend some time with them in Pennsylvania. I never met them. They both died before I was born.

"STRAIGHT ROWS OF DOUBLE HOUSES PLACED CLOSE TOGETHER, PAINTED ALL A DULL AND UGLY RED, EACH HOUSE EXACTLY LIKE ITS NEIGHBORS, SMALL BACKYARDS CLUTTERED WITH SHEDS AND PRIVIES, HOUSES AND YARDS SHOWERED WITH SMOKE AND DUST FROM THE RAILWAY AND THE BIG MINE TIPPLE – THE WHOLE SETTLEMENT ONE HIDEOUS "PATCH" ON A FAIR, OPEN HILLSIDE"

ANN ROCHESTER, "LABOR AND COAL", 1931

Continental #2 was the site of the Continental #2 Coal Mine and Coke Works owned by H.C. Frick Coke Co., a subsidiary of United States Steel. Continental #2 was not unique among the sixty plus "Patch Towns" surrounding the "Connellsville Field". This famed coal field was centered around the segment of the Pittsburgh seam that ran from Latrobe, PA to Smithfield, PA.

The coal was soft, easily mined and was nationally known as some of the finest high-volatile metallurgical coal in the world. In the early 1900's more patch towns were located in Pennsylvania than any other state in the nation.

Located on the Coal Lick Run Branch of the Pennsylvania Railroad, Continental #2 operations consisted of a bituminous

11

coal mine and 326 bee-hive coke ovens and was in operation from 1903 – 1926. Approximately 66 two story semi-detached houses, complete with outdoor privies, were built in two distinct sections along parallel streets northwest of the mine and ovens. The big house on the hill was occupied by the superintendent – "The Man". It was conveniently located on the highest point in town so he could at all time look down and observe.

The two and one half story "Company Store" was located on the main drag in the center of town. It was here that miners and their families procured the necessities of life, usually at slightly inflated prices. It was their Wal-Mart, their Super K-Mart and the only store in town. It offered everything from miner's supplies, groceries, clothing and furniture. Completing the makeup of the patch was a one story school house, baseball field and a local watering hole.

Mine management and supervision was generally under the control of the immigrants from Ireland, Scotland and England. Compassion and empathy toward the newly arrived foreigners was not one of their virtues. Miners were numbers – plain and simple. Whatever and however it took to fill hundreds of rail cars with coal and coke was all that mattered.

Miners and laborers were appropriated from the recent Ellis Island arrivals – those seeking that new lease on life in their newly adopted country. Slovaks, Poles, Czechs, Ukrainians, Hungarians were collectively referred to as "Hunkies" by their English speaking brethren – "Hunkie" being a derogatory term describing poor working immigrants of Eastern European descent.

The miners and laborers shared a common bond – survival, not only in the mines and coke ovens but in the daily life of the patch. Eastern European immigrants didn't hold a monopoly on the low end mining and coke oven positions. My Dad mentioned when growing up in Continental #2 that three Black families resided in the patch. He also mentioned that the Black workmen spoke and understood Slovak and Polish at the same time that the European immigrants were attempting to become versed in the English language. Perhaps in retrospect this was more than an act of survival than a gesture of fraternalism. It would have been advantageous for all concerned to be able to communicate with each other in the event of an emergency hundreds of feet below ground in the dark and cavernous network of mines and tunnels. Dad also mentioned that he never thought of them as Black, they were just members of the patch town family.

I'm sure that instances arose when things might have gotten out of hand at the local tavern – what else is new – alcohol has its own language. But for the most part, the language barriers and assorted ethnic idiosyncrasies aside, the "Melting Pot" of Continental #2 never boiled over.

Daily life in the patch was tough. But so were its inhabitants. Mine safety in the early 1900's was not a major concern with the powers that were. After all, those steamships from Europe were depositing replacements on the docks of the East Coast on a daily basis. Pollution was a term still many decades away in the lexicon of the populace. The ramifications of Black Lung Disease were not discovered and addressed until the 1950's. Ethnic groups of the patch tended to gravitate to their fellow countrymen to share their common language, customs and thoughts of the new world and memories of the old.

It is difficult to imagine, given today's dependence on technology how they managed to function on a daily basis – no television, no cell phone, no social media, no texting. How did they possibly get through their evening meal without a dose of

"Wheel of Fortune" or "Jeopardy"? Pat Sajak selling vowels, Vanna White turning letters, Alex Trabek uncovering the daily double – inconceivable.

For married couples the wife was usually the engine that ran the train. She paid the bills, did the shopping, cooked the meals, raised the children, planted gardens, sent her husband off to the mines with clean clothes and full lunch pail and bathed him when he returned. She also made sure that her husband didn't detour towards the tavern on payday - at least not until he deposited his meager earnings into the trusting hands of his faithful wife.

It was here in the patch town of Continental #2, located 3 miles west of Uniontown, Pennsylvania, 46 miles south of Pittsburgh, 4800 miles from Ostrov, Slovakia on Sunday, August 2, 1903 that my dad, George Van Kula was born.

CHAPTER THREE

PENNSYLVANIA TO THE MOTOR CITY

Religion was an integral element in the life of the immigrant household. The Van Kula family of Eastern Slovakia and current residents of Continental #2 were Byzantine Rite Catholics or Greek Catholics as they were often referred to at the time. In the early 1900's the nearest church catering to the Byzantine Catholics was 13 miles from Continental #2 in Leisenring, Pennsylvania. The Pennsylvania Railroad was the mode of transportation to church and back.

Dad was baptized at St. Stephen's Byzantine Catholic Church in Leisenring on August 9, 1903. Eight years later in August of 1911 St. John the Baptist Byzantine Catholic Church was established in Uniontown, PA a mere 3 miles distant from Continental #2. My grandfather was a member of the building committee. Dad, along with his siblings attended catechism classes at St. Johns on Saturdays and during the summer months. It was during one of these sojourns that one of the nuns convinced Dad to insert a space between Van and kula, and capitalize the K. Prior to this time it was spelled Vankula.

Continental #2's two room schoolhouse was the setting for Dad's only formal education - through the eighth grade. Grades

1-4 occupied one room while grades 5-8 occupied the other. Upon entering the eighth grade dad was offered the position of school custodian by his 84 year old teacher – Mr. Rhodes. He was presented with a key to the school with his duties consisting of: opening the school, starting the fire in the stove, shoveling snow, ringing the bell and making sure the hooligans (his term) got inside and seated in time for class. For his efforts he was paid $1.25 per month. Dad also mentioned he was put in charge of Room 1 (grades 1-4) on the occasions when the female teacher was late in arriving.

Prior to becoming the school custodian he would leave the house at 7 AM two to three times per week and deliver breakfast to his dad at the coke yard. He would then work with his dad for a few hours before heading off to school all with the blessing of Mr. Rhodes. During the summers he worked in the coke yard enduring the heat and noxious fumes for $3.00 per day. He was provided with a two wheeled cart and a horse named "Noble" and hauled ashes from the coke ovens to the dump. One day while backing up to the dump Noble failed to stop and landed in the pit. The supervisor and a crew of workers rescued the nag and brought her back topside. Another job saw Dad unloading 8 – 10 foot wooden posts for use in the coal mines.

Unfortunately after the eighth grade very few options were available to Dad. Higher education for a patch town kid in 1916 was not one of them. McDonalds, Burger King and Dairy Queen were light years away. He continued to work in the coke yard until the Continental #2 Coal and Coke Company ceased operations in the early 1920's. The family left the patch town behind and moved to the thriving metropolis of Uniontown, Pennsylvania 3 miles to the west.

In 1922 at the age of 19 Dad headed northeast to Woodland, Pennsylvania and The Jones and Laughlin Steel Works situated on the banks of the Ohio River. Leaving the hills of Southwestern Pennsylvania behind, Dad ventured 270 miles west to Detroit, Michigan in September of 1925. Detroit in the middle of the "Roaring Twenties" must have been an eye opener for a 22 year old Pennsylvania "Patch Kid". The population of the Motor City was over million and ranked 4th in the USA's largest cities, outranked only by New York, Chicago and Philadelphia.

The 1920's was a decade of unbridled prosperity for Detroit. The Penobscot Building, General Motors Headquarters, The Fisher Building were among the recent additions to the developing skyline. Car ferries to Windsor Canada became extinct with the opening of the Detroit-Windsor Tunnel and The Ambassador Bridge. Detroit's infamous Purple Gang was supplying liquor to the thousands of blind pigs located within the city. Ty Cobb and the Detroit Tigers were entertaining baseball fans at Michigan and Trumbull at Navin Field.

Auto production reached record levels during the 1920's and the four wheeled horseless carriage became more affordable to the masses. In 1928 Dad purchased a 1924 Ford Coupe for $85.00 thus ending his reliance on the streetcars and busses of Detroit's transit system. He was collecting a weekly paycheck and cruising city streets in his Ford Coupe - it was the twilight of the "Roaring Twenties". Things were looking up for the "Patch Town Kid".

Continental no. 2

Dad - School Pix - Continental #2 - circa 1911-1915

Dad and his 1927 Reo Victoria

Downtown Detroit - circa 1920's

SOUTHEASTERN MICHIGAN FUNERAL DIRECTORS
AND EMBALMERS ASSOCIATION, 1937-1938

"The Patch Town Kid"
Detroit - 1920's

Uniontown, Pennsylvania - 1950's Coal Mine and Coke Ovens
Original oil painting Dad's Brother - John Van Kula

CHAPTER FOUR

THE BEGINNING

The lights went out on Tuesday, October 29, 1929 when the stock market came tumbling down plunging the nation into the agony of the "Great Depression". Its ramifications descended upon Detroit with a vengeance – auto production plummeted by 40%, unemployment skyrocketed and it claimed Dad as one of its victims. Circumstances necessitated drastic measures – another change of venue was the answer.

Dad and his friend Jeff discovered an employment opportunity – in Brooklyn, New York. On July 9, 1930 Dad and Jeff arrived in the borough that was still home to the Dodgers. The employment sojourn to the Empire State lasted approximately one year and Dad returned to Detroit – this time permanently.

It was time for a career change. Dad surmised that depending on someone else for a steady paycheck may not be the best way to go. Why not control your own destiny – work for yourself- be your own boss!

How and why my Dad chose the funeral profession as his life's vocation remains a mystery. He never volunteered a reason and I never asked. Be that as it may, sometime upon his return to Detroit he began an association with the H.J. Dreyer & Co. Undertakers located at 4181 Iroquois Avenue, Detroit, MI. In retrospect it was a less than auspicious association. A component of the licensing protocol for attaining a funeral director's license in the State of Michigan in the 1930's was the serving of a two year apprenticeship under the supervision of a licensed funeral director.

He was informed by Hugh Dreyer that the apprenticeship paperwork was filed and everything was in order. For months Dad was under the impression that he was a licensed apprentice and was fulfilling licensure requirements. When it came time to contact the State of Michigan to check on his status and his next step in the procedure, Dad was informed that they had no record of his apprenticeship filing. Dreyer never filed the papers.

Dad was taken advantage of and in the process lost two years in his journey to attain a Funeral Directors License. I'm convinced that the reason for this cowardly act on Dreyer's part that knowing Dad's work ethic as I do he didn't want to lose the services of a conscientious and dedicated individual. As I mentioned in the Forward there are and were funeral directors that fell beneath the radar, in my opinion Dreyer was off the screen in 1931.

Unfortunately for Dad it was back to square one. Determined more than ever to become a licensed funeral director and embalmer he aligned himself with the J.W. McGinn Funeral Home located at 92 East Willis, Detroit, MI. This time around he personally filed his apprenticeship forms with the State of Michigan.

Serving an apprenticeship in the early 1930's in funeral service was definitely graduate school in the college of hard knocks. Days off were rarer than an English speaking tourist at Disneyland. Dad drove hearses and limousines, picked up bodies, cleaned chapels, built caskets, embalmed bodies, assisted on funeral services, washed and waxed vehicles, filed death certificates, made arrangements and other tasks vital to the 24 hour operation of a funeral home. His weekly compensation varied from week to week. He was paid $1.00 per limousine trip, which averaged out to $3.00 per week. After a period of 6 months he received a salary of $6.00 per week. He was provided "Room & Board" which consisted of a cot in the basement of the funeral home.

Old man McGinn was no dummy – he wanted his help handy. He was also treated to occasional lunches and dinners compliments of McGinn.

Dad mentioned to me that during his tenure at McGinn's he was semi-adopted by the next door neighbor. At various times during the week he would answer her knock on the basement window. Upon opening the window he would receive homemade delicacies direct from her kitchen that ranged from soups and stews to pies and cakes. He often expressed how fortunate he was for the McGinn learning experience and how thankful he was for the room and board and weekly salary during the depths of the depression, not to mention the basement window.

In 1933 Dad traded in the 1924 Ford Coupe for a 1927 Reo Victoria. With his four years of apprenticeship along with countless hours of self-study under his belt he was prepared for his final educational challenge. His objective – Pass the two day written and oral examination for the acquisition of a Michigan Funeral Director and Embalmer License. At this point in time Michigan issued two separate licenses – Funeral Director and/or Embalmer – you could acquire one or both. In 1948 The Mortuary Science Act was passed consolidating both.

In the spring of 1933 Dad aimed the Reo 90 miles Northwest out on to Grand River Avenue in the direction of Lansing, Michigan and two days of testing. The "Patch Town Kid" with the eighth grade education was successful and on June 10, 1933 was issued both a Funeral Director's and Embalmer's License in the State of Michigan. He was now his own man.

Establishing a new business has always been a risky venture, unless you were fortunate enough to have unlimited financial backing or the good fortune of attaining it through an inheritance. Dad had neither. Establishing one in the depression year of 1934 on a shoestring, a thin one at that, added immensely to the risk of failure – undeterred Dad proudly hung his funeral home establishment license on the wall where it proudly remained for the next 50 years.

His first location was at 2387 East Grand Boulevard across the street from St. Nicholas Byzantine Catholic Church. At this time he replaced the Rio with a 1931 Packard 7 Passenger Sedan. One of the prerequisites of conducting a funeral is the presence of a dead body. It would be six long months before Dad received his first death call. Within 48 hours he received his second.

Accustomed as he was to eating on a regular basis, he decided that a steady pay check would be necessary to keep the wolf from the door and creditors at bay during this initial start- up period. A position at a local manufacturing plant provided him with that weekly check. When the occasion arose to conduct a funeral, he would conveniently "become ill" until the completion of the funeral service. Less than a year after his "Grand Opening" it became economically feasible for him to shelve the factory job and devote himself full time to funeral service.

St. Nicholas Greek Catholic Church was established in Detroit in 1921 by a contingent of twenty families. Property was purchased on East Grand Boulevard, a basement church was erected in 1923 and utilized until the new church was dedicated in 1939. "St. Nicks on the Boulevard" became the catalyst for Detroit's Greek Catholic community which resided throughout metropolitan Detroit.

One of the families that joined the parish in 1924 was the family of Michael Schubeck. The history and background of the Van Kula and Schubeck families were similar in nature. Michael Schubeck was an émigré from the village of Wola Nizna near the Slovak-Polish border in the Carpathian Mountains. Anna Chomko was an émigré from the village of Zyndranowa, 11 miles west of Wola Nizna. Separately they achieved "Remarkable Journey" status as they made the trek across Europe and the Atlantic arriving in the United States in the early 1900's. Somewhere, somehow their paths crossed which eventually led to marriage vows being exchanged in 1905 in Jersey City, New Jersey. They then headed east for 300 miles and settled in the Village of St. Michael, Pennsylvania. St. Michaels was a "patch town" of the Maryland Coal Company's Maryland No. 1 mine (The deepest bituminous coal shaft in Pennsylvania). In May of 1924 they moved to Detroit, Michigan with their ten children – eight boys and two girls – one of the girls, Anne, would become my mother.

Upon arriving in the Motor City the Schubeck clan settled in on Detroit's east side at 6740 Huber Avenue, a grocery store fronting a residence in the back. Grandpa Mike was not destined to become the next grocery store tycoon as his customer IOU's steadily outnumbered his cash receivables.

George Van Kula and Anne Schubeck were married September 7, 1935 at St. Nicholas Greek Catholic Church. The reception followed at the SS. Cyril & Methodius Slovak Church hall on the corner of Heinz and Foster streets. Following a honeymoon that included visits to Niagra Falls, Washington D.C. and the family home in Uniontown, Pa they returned to Detroit to raise a family and share a life dedicated to Funeral Service. Although the legal documentation referred to the funeral home as a single proprietorship it was for all intents and purposes a "Partnership".

My mother was an integral part of the business throughout her life and contributed greatly to its success. If Dad was the pillar, then Mom was the foundation. Certain intangible attributes have to be present in a woman to become the wife of a funeral director. She managed to take first calls, ordered hearses, limousines, caskets and vaults, called in death notices and obituaries, dressed bodies, contacted doctors and hospitals, met and greeted bereaved families, set and curled the hair of deceased women, set up flowers and cleaned the chapel. In addition to the above she raised six kids in a funeral home environment, did laundry, made school lunches, cooked, baked and assisted with homework for a period of over forty years. She was also active in religious and fraternal organizations and was a loving wife, mother and grandmother. If and when they ever erect a hall of fame for funeral director's wives and moms, my Mother's in on the first ballot.

Finding the East Grand Boulevard inadequate they rented a two story home at 3128 Harper near East Grand Boulevard which served as their residence, funeral chapel and office. Funeral customs and mores in the United States have changed significantly since the 1930's. The evolution of the large modern facility designed and utilized specifically as a funeral home was still in its infancy. Detroit at this time did have a few sizable funeral establishments, but for the most part the majority were converted two story residential buildings -basically Mom and Pop operations – similar to ours.

During the 1930's and into the 1950's the majority of funerals were conducted in the home of the deceased. "Home Layouts" as they came to be known have gone the way of button shoes.

Not only was the deceased laid out in the confines of the living room, more often than not they were embalmed in their bedroom. In his capacity as an apprentice Dad assisted on many home embalming procedures. Disposing of the deceased's blood via the bathroom plumbing wasn't one of his favorite tasks but as he remarked – "Someone had to do it". It tasks my thought process to the limit as to how "bedroom embalming" was accomplished in the days before air conditioning – as a matter of fact how it was done at all. But the pioneers of funeral service carried on and embalming was eventually transferred to the prep rooms of the modern funeral home.

McGinn Funeral Home
92 East Willis, Detroit, Michigan Dad's apprenticeship 1931-1933

GEORGE   VAN KULA
FUNERAL   DIRECTOR
Slovenský Pohrábnik

3128 Harper Ave.   PLaza 4370
Near E. Grand Blvd.   Detroit, Mich.

GEORGE VAN KULA
FUNERAL HOME
A Service Within
Your Means

We always help the bereaved family to avoid unnecessary expense but we make no compromise in the quality of materials or the thoroughness of our work.

Our service is complete in every respect. Nothing ever is overlooked. Nothing is left for the bereaved family to do. Every detail cared for — knowingly, helpfully and comfortingly.

You always may be certain of this, regardless of the cost of the service you select. Anyway, you be sure that we will as let you to have arrangements for an appropriate funeral that will be within your means.

2387 E. Grand Blvd.
DETROIT

Phone: MAdison 2287

First Ad - 1934

COMPLIMENTS OF

Geo. Van Kula
FUNERAL DIRECTOR

Phone: PLaza 4370

3128 Harper Ave.   Detroit

::: Compliments of :::

George Van Kula
Funeral Home

9074 ST. CYRIL   Tel.: PLaza 4370

Telefon: WAlnut 1-4370

Pozdravuje a zdaru želá 18. konvencii Živeny

GEORGE VAN KULA

Slovenský pohrebník a balzamovač

9074 ST. CYRIL,   DETROIT 13
nárožie *Marcus*   MICHIGAN

CHAPTER FIVE

THE 1940'S

As the decade of the 1930's drew to a close Harper Avenue began to experience growing pains. The funeral operation was steadily improving and the family increased by two with the arrival of my brother and sister. Mom and Dad were exploring their options in regards to relocating when fate intervened. A funeral home was on the market. Not only was it on the market, but the market was in Detroit's Slovak neighborhood. It was directly across the street from SS. Cyril & Methodius Slovak Catholic Church. A match made in Heaven. How fortuitous!

The Petrik Funeral Home located at 9074 St. Cyril Avenue, Detroit, MI ceased operations in 1941. Dad acquired the deed and relocated in January of 1942. The Van Kula Funeral Home at the corner of St. Cyril and Marcus would faithfully serve the neighborhood for the next 36 years.

9074 St. Cyril was a two story, yellow brick, two-family-residence built in 1928. The street was originally named Centerline Avenue and sometime in the 1930's it was renamed St.Cyril Avenue – the Slovak Pastor had some clout at City Hall. The first floor contained the funeral chapel and office, the second floor was home. The basement was divided into three areas – smoking lounge, supply room and laundry area. The prep room or morgue was located in the rear of the two car garage - the backyard – nonexistent.

St. Cyril Avenue was approximately one mile in length and ran north and south from Harper to Van Dyke. Spaced 40 feet apart, magnificent Dutch Elm trees bordered the asphalt for its entire length. Nothing signaled the onset of spring more than the budding and blossoming of the Dutch Elms. And nothing heralded the approach of winter more than their golden leaves cascading down from their branches where they were raked and swept into mounds. Some neighbors opted to set their mounds ablaze sending plumes of aromatic smoke into the autumn sky. It still remains one of the most cherished memories of a Midwestern fall – the smell of burning leaves. Unfortunately the majority of St.Cyril's Dutch Elm's fell victim to Dutch-Elm disease that ravaged Detroit's 400,000 Elms beginning in the 1950's and left many neighborhoods barren and exposed – a fateful harbinger of Detroit's future.

In the 1940's Detroit's East Side, more specifically the Harper-Van Dyke area was about as "Blue Collar" as any neighborhood in the nation. It was also home to an ethnic collage of Slovaks, Poles, Italians and Germans. European immigrants didn't hold a monopoly on the ethnic composition of the Harper-Van Dyke neighborhood. Although the inhabitants of the rolling hills of Eastern Europe and Southwestern Pennsylvania were well represented, migrants from the rolling hills of Appalachia added to the diversification of Detroit's East Side.

Today 7301 Harper Avenue, corner of Field, one block west of St. Cyril Avenue lies vacant, littered with urban trash and overgrown with out of control vegetation. In the 1940's a service station and the Detroit terminal of The Brooks Bus Line occupied the corner lot. Headquartered in Paducah, Kentucky Brooks served as the transportation conduit between Detroit and Western Kentucky. For over 40 years it transported workers and their families north to the auto plants of in the words of Bobby Bare – "Detroit City". "But by day I make the cars, by night I make the bars". I vividly recall the hundreds of times I drove by that corner and now many years later can only speculate as to the personal anecdotes of those present on their journeys on the "Paducah Express". How many of those southerners remained in the North? How did the social assimilation with their European neighbors play out? How many permanently returned on the "Express" to the pastoral solitude of Paducah on the banks of the Ohio River?

St. Cyril and Marcus was 11 blocks north of Harper and 1 block west of Van Dyke and approximately 5 miles from downtown Detroit. Harper and Van Dyke were both vibrant commercial thoroughfares – Van Dyke running North and South and Harper East and West. The anchor of the Harper-Van Dyke intersection was the Eastown Theater located at 8041 Harper just east of Van Dyke. Built in the late 1920's it opened for business on October 1, 1931. Clark Gable headlined a movie titled "Sporting Blood"- A title in retrospect that was most ironic considering the future fate of the Harper-Van Dyke area. Actually it was more than a high end movie house with an imported marble lobby and stairway and gold gilded ceiling. It housed offices, stores, 35 apartments in addition to its "Grand Ballroom" with its oak dance floor and extravagant band shell. A multitude of retail establishments encompassed the Harper-Van Dyke area in the pre-mall era of the 1940's: Cunningham's Drug Store, Van Dyke Theater, Harper Recreation, White Tower Restaurant, Federal's Department Store, Woolworth's, Neisner's, Kresge's, Club Stevedora, Sanders, Catholic Supply House to mention a few.

An integral criteria of the immigrant's choice of neighborhood, beside the proximity to his place of employment, was the church. Ethnic conclaves sprung up throughout the city as incoming workers gravitated to the area of "their people" and "their church". An addition to the neighborhood mix were ethnic social clubs, fraternal organizations, markets, bakeries and of course – the beer garden.

There were no shortages of beer gardens or bars in the ethnic neighborhoods of the Motor City. The Harper-Van Dyke area was no exception. I vividly remember a few neighborhood intersections where a watering hole sat prominently on every corner. The majority of 1940 neighborhood dwellings did not possess dens, family rooms or finished basements. Television was in its infancy, "Man Caves" were light years away and the radio provided the household entertainment. Thus, outside of one's living room or the kitchen table, the local beer garden was adopted as the social entity of the ethnic neighborhood. Friday Fish Fry's, traditional ethnic foods, weekend dancing, along with blue collar comradery were the enticements of your local beer garden. As the Philco's, Admiral's and Motorola's hit the shelves in the late 1940's beer gardens were some of the first to exhibit the images of the television screen. Televised Friday Night Fights were a big draw in the bar rooms of America. The bar became the "Old Man's" refuge after an eight or ten hour day of popping engine blocks into Plymouths, Packard's or Hudson's. Nothing like a shot or two of "Four Roses", "7 Crown" or "Old Crow" washed down with a schuper or boomba of ice cold "Pfeiffer's" or "E&B" after a hard day on the line.

Speaking of "Old Crow", problems arose on the home front when "Pops" would overstay his welcome on the bar stool and "Mama" would dispatch one of the kids in his direction and escort him home. If by chance it happened to be payday, nine times out of ten, "Mama" herself would make the journey.

Detroit's population was increasing at a fairly substantial rate in the early 1940's and would drastically increase with the advent of World War II. A significant addition of citizenry to the Motor City census rolls emanated from the coal mines and coke ovens of Southwest Pennsylvania. The auto plants offered somewhat safer working conditions and a more reliable income. They were trading the pollution of the "Patch Towns" for the pollution of the auto plants.

Chrysler Corporation's Plymouth Lynch Road Assembly Plant designed by Albert Kahn opened in 1929. In the 1940's it was the largest automobile plant in the world employing over 12,000 workers. During World War II production shifted to manufacturing 40 MM aircraft guns. In 1943 they became involved with "Top Secret Project X-100" part of the Manhattan Project (the effort to develop the atomic bomb) and produced diffusers which were shipped to Oak Ridge, Tennessee. Lynch Road Assembly was less than a mile from 9074 St. Cyril Avenue.

Located between Huber Avenue and Lynch Road the plant stretched out on the east side of Mt. Elliott for approximately one half mile. On the west side of Mt. Elliott across the street from the plant were homes some of which were turned into bars for the benefit of the thirsty auto workers. The enterprising inhabitants created beer gardens with a shot and a beer as the cash crop. In an effort to conserve as much of the worker's allotted break time or lunch hour, shots and beers were lined up the entire length of the bar. When that lunch or break time whistle sounded a mass of humanity bolted from the factory across Mt. Elliott to the awaiting libations. Pity the poor driver traversing Mt. Elliott at the time as he was engulfed by thirsty auto workers as they headed for happy hour.

Packard Motor Car Company – Detroit was located on East Grand Boulevard and Connor and was another Albert Kahn design. In 1942 car production was halted as manufacturing efforts were focused on producing Rolls Royce airplane engines and PT boat engines for the US Navy. Packard Motor Car Company was 1 ½ miles from 9074 St. Cyril Avenue.

Chrysler Corporation's Dodge Main was located on Joseph Campau in Hamtramck, MI on the northern outskirts of Detroit. Several of the buildings in the complex were designed by Albert Kahn. The first Dodge rolled off the line in 1914. During World War II Dodge Main and its 44,000 workers were manufacturing military trucks and ambulances. Dodge Main was 2 miles from 9074 St. Cyril Avenue.

I'm sure that somewhere in the confines of Nazi Germany there existed in some obscure secret intelligence headquarters a map of my neighborhood with its multitude of war manufacturing operations duly highlighted – we were definitely in the crosshairs of "The Arsenal of Democracy".

This was the configuration and backdrop of the "HOOD" as of March, 1943. I became part of it on Tuesday morning, March 2, making my grand entrance at Detroit's Harper Hospital as duly reported on the front page of the "Eastown-Nortown News". Dad was uptight with the publisher - either that or they were starved for news. As I was transported home in the family Packard little did I realize that 9074 St. Cyril would not only be my residence but also of my future employment.

Perhaps the first indication that I lived in a diverse environment entered my four year old mind sometime in 1947. World War II was in the history books, Comrade Stalin was still planting the hammer and sickle throughout Europe and the auto companies were manufacturing cars once again instead of tanks and ammunition. The majority of service men and women had returned from the shores of Europe and the Pacific to a different America, including my five uncles and one aunt.

The Van Kula and Schubeck families were thanking God for the safe return of the family members from tours of duty in the European and Pacific theaters of war. The blue star service flag was proudly displayed in the window of the Schubeck residence on St. Clair street with its four blue stars indicating that my grandmother had four sons serving in World War II. Uncle Charlie, Mom's youngest brother, graduated from Southeastern High School in June of 1944. January 1, 1945 he was sailing on the Queen Mary with the US Army 6th Cavalry headed for Europe. His brother Paul served in the US Army and was in the European Theater of Operations. Brother Pete was in the South Pacific with the US Navy and Brother Frank was aboard a US Navy destroyer. On the Van Kula side, Dad's younger brother John and sister Ann returned to Uniontown, Pennsylvania at the end of hostilities. Uncle John was inducted into the US Army on 11 NOV 42 at the age of 37. He endured over 150 days of combat in France and Germany and was awarded the Bronze Star. At the age of 34 Aunt Ann was a member of the US Army Nurse Corps and was assigned duty at the 54th General Hospital in Hollandia, Dutch New Guinea.

One day my four year old legs were traversing the myriad steps and rooms of the funeral home when I encountered Dad and another gentleman placing a man in a casket. Of course the man in the casket was dead, whatever that meant. My house possessed all the ingredients and trappings of a special type of place. It had lots of rooms, lots of stairs, lots of character, and at certain times throughout its existence - characters. My house was one of the largest in the neighborhood, but to the uninitiated and curious it possessed a certain aura – it had dead bodies in it. Didn't every house contain caskets and dead bodies? This four year old thought so. But just to be sure I had to check it out with my main man at time, Danny. Danny lived three doors down from the funeral home on Marcus. We checked out his basement but all we found was a coal bin and some old furniture and stuff – no dead bodies. Of course the care free days of the 1940's are no more. It wouldn't surprise me that there were more than a few dead bodies discovered in the basements of Marcus Street in the ensuing years of Detroit's drug and gang wars.

Growing up with death alleviated any fears I may have harbored concerning our frequent house guests. Having a dead person around when I was a kid was as natural to me as the Cleveland Indians being 24 games out of first place by the Fourth of July. At this point in time it was quite prevalent for families to reside over their place of business. One of my childhood chums had the good fortune of residing over the family beer garden. The only difference between his place and ours was that in our place you came in "stiff".

Being raised over a funeral home was unique to say the least. Sharing that experience with three brothers and two sisters added to the kaleidoscope of daily events. Dull moments were few and far between, although at times I believed my parents yearned for the few. I don't believe Dr. Spock had a chapter in his book entitled "Raising Six Kids in a Funeral Home". If he was so inclined my dear mother could have penned it for him.

Actress and singer Ann-Margret is one of the most famous and well known entertainers of my generation. I'm sure she is totally unaware of the fact that we share something in common. In 1952 she resided in a funeral home in Wilmette, Illinois. Too bad it wasn't the one on St. Cyril Avenue in Detroit. I would have traded in my two sisters and my baseball card collection for that deal. Commenting on her three year funeral home experience Ann-Margret replied "It wasn't at all spooky".

The house on St. Cyril erected in 1928 contained wooden floors, plaster walls and ceilings – it was not soundproof. Throughout the course of time the upstairs floor took on a character of its own manifested in squeaks and creaks and much to Dad's chagrin these upstairs sounds reverberated downward. Consequently when the downstairs' funeral chapel was occupied our family movements and life style were somewhat restricted – no running, radio (later to include television) volume set at minimum levels, no sibling wrestling, no boisterous conversations and my least favorite – no hockey games on the kitchen floor. During periods of chapel occupancy, the home sweet home environment of the upper residence took on an almost monastic air. There were times I believed I resided in a church or monastery – the only trappings missing were the bells and vigil lights.

One of the bulletin board maxims adorning one of my grade school classrooms read "SILENCE IS GOLDEN". I believe to this day that Dad persuaded or paid off one of the nuns to display it. A parental exhortation that still permeates my subconscious to this day was – "Quiet, there are people downstairs". Although we didn't relish those days and nights of restricted behavior, we learned to adjust and live with them. As we got older we realized that by the downstairs chapel being occupied that it added to the family coffers – thus making available to us the necessities of life in the form of food, clothing, shelter and trading cards.

In those periods when the downstairs was void of mourners a semblance of normalcy returned to the upper environs of the funeral home. The radio or TV increased in volume, footsteps returned to a normal cadence and face offs returned to the kitchen floor. We never knew when the "QUIET" sign would reappear. We did know that people died at anytime and anywhere. We also knew that Dad was on call 24/7. The celebration of holidays, birthdays, family outings, special events were all subject to revision depending on the random ring of the phone or doorbell.

Not long after the Thanksgiving turkey was history I began a litany of pleas – "Can we set up the trains now"? I was always given the same reply – "When we put up the tree". Mom and Dad were hard line traditionalists of the old country school of Christmas decorating – a week before Christmas. Step number one was a trip to the Eastern Market to obtain a Douglas fir. For as long as I can recollect my Dad was under the assumption we had a 12' high living room ceiling and bought accordingly. Of course we only had an 8' ceiling which annually created a myriad of technical issues. Among them was my Mother's wish not to alter the top or bottom branches.

Eventually upon the completion of the emotional alterations in the basement, the tree was transported up four flights of stairs to the living room. It didn't end there. Getting the tree to stand in an upright position and remain that way often took a series of adjustments. The one that always seemed to work was wiring it to the window.

Once in place, a multitude of boxes would be carted down from the attic. To me the only ones that mattered were the ones that contained the Lionels. As soon as the angel took up her position on the top of the Douglas Fir I promptly began assembling train and track - wasn't long before they were steaming around tree. Unfortunately bedtime arrived much too soon. But there was always tomorrow when I would once again take up my position as chief engineer of the family railroad. Inevitably the inevitable occurred – someone had died during the night. It was back to "Silence is Golden" and the trains sat idly at the station until chapel visiting hours concluded. This unfortunately was past my bed time of the era – another cruel blow for the "Funeral Director's Son".

Dogs bark so they were quickly eliminated in the family pet selection categories. An exception to the "No Dogs" policy occurred on March 2, 1947 when someone decided that I should have a dog for my fourth birthday - enter "Blinker", a black cocker spaniel. Actually his tenure on St. Cyril was short lived. After a few weeks it was decided that he would take up residence with my widowed Grandma Schubeck. In retrospect I believe this was the plan all along.

Grandma Schubeck and Uncle Charlie built the first house on Bringard Street in the area of 8 Mile and Kelly in Northeast Detroit. The area still contained farms and was for the most part undeveloped. As a matter of fact the farmer across Kelly Road would bring produce to my grandmother – his farmland would later be the site of Eastland Shopping Center, Notre Dame and Regina High Schools. Kelly Road was still unpaved from 7 Mile to 8 Mile. A housing development was being constructed on the block behind Grandma's house. One afternoon she called Blinker from his romp in the backyard to come in the house. He was never seen again. Uncle Charlie and Grandma believed he was dognapped by one of the construction crew. I hope he was given a good home.

Over a period of time rabbits, gold fish, baby chicks and kittens comprised the pet category that joined the sibling fraternity on St. Cyril Avenue. One kitten in particular made a lasting family impression, especially on my Dad. "Macka" (Slovak for cat) – my Mom named them all "Macka", was intent on testing the nine lives

41

theory. He was a wanderer, which posed no problem when the chapel was vacant. One afternoon he decided to pay his respects to the deceased lying in state on the first floor. Once his absence from the living quarters was discovered, "General Quarters" was sounded. We had it down to a science – the kids would make a thorough search of the attic, stairways and basement. Failing in our attempt to locate the missing feline, it fell upon Mom to complete the search and rescue mission – it was her task to search the chapel.

As she made her way downstairs in a state of embarrassment she was hoping that her furry little friend was back upstairs under a bed. Due to the hour of the afternoon, visitation was minimal, a fact which Mom was thankful for. Scanning the length of the room she observed the deceased's brother in law on all fours amidst the flower arrangements at the head of the casket. Not a good sign. He retrieved the cowering Macka and handed him to Mom with a smile on his face. All was well, except for Macka who was immediately put on the endangered species list by my Dad. I wonder if he signed the register- book?

My initiation into the family business began at an early age and was a gradual process. About the age of four I occasionally accompanied Dad as he traversed the city obtaining death certificates and securing burial permits. This was pre-freeway days and travel was restricted to city thoroughfares. I vividly recall traveling on the Davison Freeway, the first urban freeway constructed in the United States. It opened in 1942 and substantially reduced Dad's crosstown travel time. Dad introduced me to the businessman's lunch – whenever possible we stopped for a White Tower hamburger and orange pop. Seven decades later I still consider the White Tower burger to be the preeminent patty ever to slide off a grill - unfortunate that they went the way of the button shoe.

In addition to being a travel companion to Dad, I was soon bestowed with another role – resident altar boy. An integral ritual of the Byzantine Catholic burial proceedings is the "Parastas" – a memorial service normally held at the funeral home the night before the church services the following day. The pastor and cantor officiated in front of the casket. At the age of four Mom presented me with my own custom made black cassock. My official altar boy duties were to assist the priest by holding the kadilo (an ornamental container for burning incense) and the holy water sprinkler - pretty heady stuff for a kid a few months away from entering kindergarten.

One of the difficulties I experienced was the inhalation of the smoke drifting up from the kadilo – at the conclusion of the thirty minute service I could hold my own with any of the smoked sausages at the Hungarian meat market. As a four year old I was often beset with sporadic periods of boredom. Services were chanted in Church Slavonic, one of the most beautiful and uplifting melodies in religious rituals. This was especially true when being sung by an entire chapel of family and friends. It is a service that throughout the passage of time I have grown to admire and love- but at the age of four I would have opted for the condensed version.

At the conclusion of the service the priest blessed the deceased with holy water and he and the assembled mourners sang the memorial hymn, "Vicnaja Pamat" (Eternal Memory). I realized even then that this was moment that unlocked the emotional storage vault of the family and if there were any fainters in attendance this was their cue. As the first few notes of "Vicnaja Pamat" filled the air I found myself scanning the crowd for any potential droppers – a habit that would exist during my years in funeral service and with my hand cradling the silk covered glass capsule of smelling salts.

One of Dad's favorite anecdotes which he enjoyed sharing on numerous occasions concerned an incident that transpired at the conclusion of a funeral home memorial service. I was dutifully holding the holy water sprinkler when the moment arrived for the final blessing. Father Sabow extended his hand to me expecting that would hand him the sprinkler – I didn't. I shook his hand. Although Dad may not have realized it at the time, this was a significant public relations gesture on my part. In funeral service it is prudent to foster positive relations with members of the cloth.

My altar boy career spanned a period of 14 years and encompassed two rites of the Catholic Church – Byzantine and Roman. I began assisting at St. Nicholas' Byzantine Rite Liturgy at the age of four and at St.Cyril's Roman Rite masses in the seventh grade. Occasions arose during the St. Cyril school year when I would be scheduled to serve a Funeral Mass. This was a highly sought after and prized assignment for it entailed an absence from morning classes. It sure beat diagramming sentences.

Although the Van Kula Funeral Home was an eastside entity, Dad's clientele was not confined to any geographic area. By virtue of his being referred to as "Slovenske Pohrebnik" (Slovak Funeral Director) and his membership in various civic and fraternal organizations his sphere of service encompassed the entire City of Detroit. He was a founding member and eventual president of The Pennsylvania Club of Detroit, a social organization consisting of natives of the Keystone State now residing in the Motor City. During its peak years it boasted a membership of over two thousand transplanted Pennsylvanians. He was also a member and officer of the Harper-Van Dyke Businessmen's Association and Detroit Exchange Club. He served on the Board of Directors of the Greek Catholic Union, Financial Secretary of St. Nicholas Church and was a member and President of District One of the Michigan Funeral Directors Association - Quite a resume for the "Patch Town Kid".

During the 1940's "The Slovak Funeral Director" served families and conducted funerals in a cross section of Detroit's neighborhoods including: St. Stephen's Byzantine Catholic Church on Thaddeus Street in Delray, St. Wenceslaus (Bohemian) on St. Antoine, Detroit, Slovak Baptist Church on Harper Ave., Detroit, Holy Ghost Carpatho-Russian Church on Mound Road, Detroit, SS. Cyril & Methodius Slovak Church, St. Cyril Avenue, Detroit, St. Nicholas Byzantine Catholic Church, East Grand Boulevard, Detroit, Holy Name Church, Van Dyke, Detroit, Patronage of St. Joseph Church, Georgia Street, Detroit, St. Thomas the Apostle Church, Miller Avenue, Detroit, Resurrection Catholic Church, Miller Ave., Detroit, Bethany Lutheran Church, Outer Drive, Detroit. Protestant Services were often conducted from the funeral home on St. Cyril Avenue.

During the 1930's up until the late 1960's Detroit's Catholic-Ethnic congregations were at their zenith. Dozens of churches, rectories, schools and gyms were still operational throughout Detroit neighborhoods. One or more funeral homes were usually located in close proximity to the parish complex - its owner generally reflecting the same ethnicity of the majority of parish membership. By virtue of their proximity to the church, along with their ethnic affiliation they were often referred to as "The Parish Funeral Director".

At this point in time certain priests guarded their fiefdoms much in the same manner as the lords of feudal England. They exerted a much greater influence and control of their flock than the clergy of today. It was their way or the highway. They resented any intrusions on their authority and or sphere of influence. At times these intrusions occurred when certain families opted through their own free will to select a funeral director other than the one that was connected to the parish. These acts of treason were met head on by the pastor and often involved a verbal rebuke to the family or an act of intimidation directed toward the interloping funeral director.

Dad was a recipient of a few of these acts of clergy unchristian behavior. In one instance upon arriving at the church in advance of the funeral procession he found the main church doors locked. Entering an open side door he made his way to the vestibule of the church and opened the doors. He then led the funeral cortege out of the inclement elements of a winter morning, into the vestibule of the darkened church and waited. They waited in silence and darkness.

After a period of five embarrassing minutes lights were turned on, altar boys appeared and lit candles and the holy man of the cloth begrudgingly ambled to the vestibule to begin the service. Following the conclusion at the cemetery of services the immediate family approached Dad and offered their apologies for the narrow mindedness of their pastor.

On another occasion of being cast in the role of outsider the priest berated Dad in front of the family and mourners for arriving late for the church service. Anticipating some type of priestly ploy and being forewarned by the family of the priest's displeasure of George Van Kula handling the funeral, Dad and the funeral cortege arrived at the church ten minutes early.

When a death occurred in certain parishes and the pastor was present he did everything but dial the number of the parish funeral director. What possessed these pious men of the cloth to profess such allegiance to their local funeral director? Were they of the impression that "their man" conducted a funeral service with more dignity than anyone else? Did they believe their parish funeral home was more aesthetically appealing than any other? Was it ethnic loyalty? Some of the above may have been true but rumor had it that some were on the take.

"Home Layouts" were still in vogue in the 1940's and into the 1950's as families opted to have the funeral viewing in the confines of the family residence – a throwback to their European roots. It wasn't uncommon for Dad to arrange and direct funerals within a radius of 12 miles from 9074 St. Cyril.

Transforming a residence into a makeshift funeral chapel was a logistical and formidable undertaking. (No pun intended – on second thought it was). One of the first orders of business was the transformation of the residential living room to create as much space as possible by the rearranging and elimination of furniture. A flowered mourning wreath was ordered for the front door that acted as a silent symbol to the neighborhood of the recent death of an occupant. A service company would arrive at the house with a floor covering and a set of palms. Dad and his crew would make the trip from the funeral home to the residence transporting: back drapes, candle holders, kneeler, register stand, Mass card holder, torchiere funeral floor lamps, standing crucifix, flower stands, bier catafalque, church-truck and folding chairs.

Once everything was in the place the moment arrived for the deceased to enter the home for the final time. This was generally the most precarious operation depending on the architectural configuration of the house and the size and weight of the casket. Wooden porch steps and porches presented the first obstacle. Back in the day the majority of them were coated with grey oil based paint which often gave rise to slipping and sliding, especially in inclement weather. The front door was usually removed to garner an additional few precious inches of clearance.

Eventually the casket would find its way into the living room – but not always through the front door. Somewhere in the City of Detroit stands or in all probability once stood, is a house attesting to the ingenuity of my father. Unable to maneuver the casket through the front door for whatever reason, he executed Plan B – the removal of the window frame. Once the casket was maneuvered through opening, the window frame was replaced. On the morning of the funeral the procedure was reversed. Dad's credo – "Nothing is Impossible".

Detroit houses were not all single family dwellings - a fair section of them were two story two family habitats. Upper flat home layouts added another dimension to the course of action necessary for the successful completion of getting the casket into the living room. Conquering the dozen or more stairs of the narrow stairway was only the first step. Reaching the top usually required that the casket be placed on end and maneuvered through the doorway into the living quarters. In addition all of the equipment essential for a home layout had to be transported up. Upper flat layouts weren't for the faint hearted or physically fragile.

Family members were normally absent as these preparations were in progress. Sometimes they congregated at a neighbor's home or an out of sight location of their own. Dad and his assistant opened the casket and ascertained how the body survived the trip from the funeral home, up the stairs, through the door or window frame to its place in the living room. Upon completion of the necessary adjustments to the remains and satisfied that everything was in order Dad would summon the family to the casket – the funeral was on.

Family and friends knelt at the casket, offered a prayer, signed the register book and shared memories of the recently departed. The kitchen became a beehive of activity as homemade delicacies were delivered to the home by relatives and neighbors. More often than not a makeshift back porch or basement bar would provide alcohol for those so inclined.

Dad's responsibilities didn't end with the first viewing. He remained to set up and arrange incoming floral arrangements, attempting to see that all seats had chairs and to resolve any problems that may arise. A favorite anecdote he enjoyed sharing about the "old days" concerned air conditioning or the lack thereof. Some Michigan summer days can be notorious and oppressive in regards to their elevated levels of temperature and humidity. For just such occasions Dad purchased a portable fan cooler. A large block of ice was deposited in the unit, turned on and the electric fan circulated cool air throughout the room. At times its positive effects generated negative consequences. As the crowded room cooled off those inside were prone to stay inside. Thus those mourners outside were forced to remain outside until there was adequate space available inside for them to enter.

Dedicated and successful funeral directors had to possess the ability to think quickly and astutely. Quickly realizing that no attempt was being made by the "insiders" to exit, Dad made his move – hopefully unnoticed he sauntered over to the cooler and pulled the plug. Within minutes the comfort level dropped dramatically and those present headed for the door and a "breath of fresh air". A fresh throng of mourners would enter the home the cooling unit would mysteriously start up and would remain so until circumstances warranted another "breakdown".

Home layout visitation generally lasted anywhere from one to three days with two days being the average. Saturday was the most popular day of choice for a funeral service with various factors in play that lead to this option. Out of town family members planning on attending the services were limited at the time in the mode of transportation available to them. Air travel was in its infancy, thus leaving them the choice of auto, bus or train as their mode of transportation. During World War II travel was extremely restricted throughout the United States a factor which entered into the decision of the family in the selection of the day of the funeral service. Also Saturday was generally a day off in the work force and wouldn't necessitate losing a day's wages to attend a funeral. Saturday funerals weren't always possible but every effort was made to accede to the wishes and desires of the family.

Prior to the day of burial Dad had to acquire a completed death certificate, file it with the appropriate government agency and secure a burial permit. At times perhaps the most difficult of these tasks was securing the completion and signing of the medical portion of the death certificate. This portion of the legal document was to be filled out and signed by the deceased's attending physician, or in the absence of one, the Medical Examiner. This process could consume 2-3 hours or more depending on distances involved and the cooperation or not of the attending physician. Then it was back to the residence of the deceased to supervise visitation and attend to the final details relating to the morning of the service. Dad was conspicuously absent from home during the periods of those home layouts.

As in football every funeral service had a "Game Plan" – to synchronize and coordinate the specifics in regards to church services, route of funeral procession to church and cemetery, parking, transportation involving family and clergy and have a plan "B" in place to address any unforeseen situations that may occur.

The forming of a funeral procession on one of Detroit's residential streets was not an easy accomplishment. The afternoon prior to the funeral Dad would post "NO PARKING – FUNERAL" signs up and down the street adjacent to the home of the deceased. Sometimes they worked – sometimes they didn't. It paid to be on good terms with your neighbor or he might not move his car for your funeral. Detroit residential streets allowed parking on one side of the street both sides or no parking at all. Hopefully space could be provided in front of the residence for the hearse, flower car, limousine with the family and friends vehicles directly behind. The procession line up became more chaotic during the winter months whenever a snowfall contributed an additional obstacle.

The morning of the funeral the priest arrived and officiated at a brief service followed by those in attendance passing by the casket to pay their final respects – the members of the immediate family were the last to approach the casket. Eastern European women possessed a high degree of volatility in their external display of emotion which often times manifested itself at the final farewell. Dad always strategically placed himself at the head of the casket to be in a position to assist in the case of an impulsive act of emotion. There were times when these acts included the distraught widow leaning into the casket and grabbing her husband by the shoulders and nearly knocking the casket off the church truck but the more common occurrence was fainting. Dad may have left home without his American Express Card but he never left for a funeral without the smelling salts.

Once family and friends were safely ensconced in their vehicles Dad and his assistant closed the casket and summoned the pallbearers. Pallbearers came in all shapes and sizes – they were often relatives, close friends, neighbors or co-workers. There were times when the task of pall- bearing affected certain individuals emotionally and they found a visit to the back porch or basement bar for a snort or two of "Old Crow" a beneficial antidote for their condition. As the pallbearers navigated the doorway, steps and sidewalks and safely placed the casket in the hearse they joined the others in their vehicles. The cortege slowly pulled away from the deceased's home one final time and proceeded to the church and cemetery – the home layout was history.

What goes up must come down. Once the casket and mourners were en route to the church from the family residence it was time to restore the home to its pre-funeral setting. Dad would employ a one or two man crew to arrive at the home and transfer the equipment previously deployed back to the funeral home. If it happened to be a Saturday service more than likely I was on the receiving end of the transfer and assisted in unloading and securing all items in their proper storage area.

I recall one incident of a "breakdown" sometime in the 1950's that garnered the interest of The Detroit Police Department. The family had returned to their residence after the completion of the funeral services and shortly thereafter noticed that the deceased's coin collection was missing. Dad was contacted and the detective's first thoughts were directed to the service company employees that removed the funeral equipment from the home during the church services. Upon further investigation it was determined that one of the grandsons stopped by and lifted the coins - evidently he couldn't wait for the reading of the will.

"My First Day on the Job"
Brother George, Me, Sister Rosemary. We each had our own shovel.

Me and "Blinker" Grandma Schubeck's
backyard - 1947 Prior to the "Dognapping"

Dad and I sporting our
1947 Easter threads!

Dad and Emory Metzger 1943 - layout World War II - no metal caskets

The "infamous" leaded glass windows and doors "Where are they NOW?"

February, 1947 - St. Nicholas Church - altar boy duty.

June, 1949-St Cyril Kindergarten Graduation

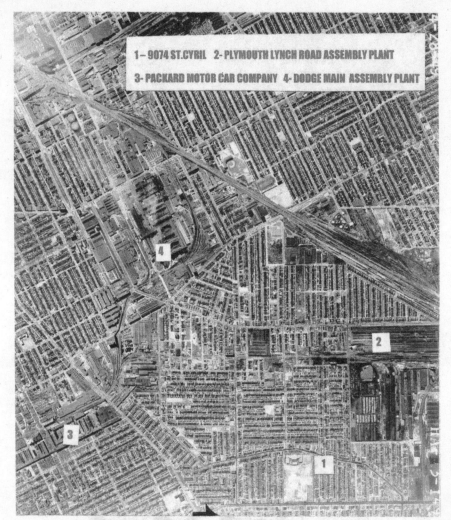

1– 9074 ST.CYRIL   2- PLYMOUTH LYNCH ROAD ASSEMBLY PLANT

3- PACKARD MOTOR CAR COMPANY   4- DODGE MAIN ASSEMBLY PLANT

THE 'HOOD" --- APRIL 28, 1949

LYNCH ROAD ASSEMBLY PLANT

THESE WERE
THE AUTO PLANTS
OF MY
NEIGHBORHOOD -
WON'T YOU BE
MY NEIGHBOR?

1956 DUAL GHIA

MYSTERY PRANKS

Couple Receives a Flood of Unordered Disorder

Somebody with a highly fertile imagination and a deeply rooted grudge against George and Ann Van Kula is rapidly driving them to the border of hysteria.

The Van Kulas, who operate an undertaking establishment at 9074 St. Cyril, sought the help of police today in tracking down the person or persons responsible for the flood of telephone calls, merchandise deliveries, flat seekers and job applicants that have made their life a nightmare since last Wednesday.

The trouble began when a veterinarian arrived to care for the dog the Van Kulas do not own.

THEN THE DELUGE

In rapid succession, a man arrived with a juke box they did not order, two towcars arrived for their unwrecked car and a truck came with a typewriter they did not want.

Two television repairmen, two exterminator company employes, a floor sanding worker, two coal trucks loaded to the top, two barbecued chickens and five gallons of ice cream had to be turned away Thursday, Friday and Saturday.

But the real trouble came Sunday. The Van Kulas' nemesis had advertised in two newspapers that their upstairs flat was for rent, cheap, and that they wanted a handyman, wages good.

SIGN OF DESPERATION

First came the line of flat-seekers, money in hand and eager to see the Van Kulas' flat, which is over the funeral parlor.

The line of jobseekers was even longer and voluble than the line of flatseekers. In desperation, Mrs. Van Kula tacked a placard on the door and started to explain the hoax in big black letters.

She finished by scratching out the explanation and writing, in letters of exhausted deception: "Job is Filled."

Detectives said the Van Kulas could offer no clue to their tormentor.

MRS. ANN VAN KULAS
Victim of Prankster

HENRY FORD'S LAST RIDE
"PACKARD HEARSE"

CHAPEL VISITING HOURS 10AM TO 11PM

VISITING HOURS - 1930'S - 1940'S

1954 CADILLAC FLOWER CAR

CHAPTER SIX

WORLD WAR II

December 7, 1941 "That date which will live in infamy" changed the world, the way we lived and the way we buried our dead.

IN DEEP AND EVERLASTING APPRECIATION OF THE HEROIC EFFORTS OF THOSE WHO, IN KEEPING THEIR COUNTRY FREE, MADE THE SUPREME SACRIFICE IN WORLD WAR II, THE ENTIRE NATION HAS BEEN DEDICATED TO DISPOSING OF THE MORTAL REMAINS OF THOSE HONORED DEAD IN A MANNER CONSISTENT WITH THE WISHES OF THEIR NEXT OF KIN

HARRY S. TRUMAN
PRESIDENT OF THE UNITED STATES

In the 1940's Detroit bound railroad passengers arrived at either The Michigan Central Station on 15th Street and Vernor Highway or Union Depot located on West Fort Street and Third Street. Michigan Central was handling over 4,000 passengers daily and a lesser amount at the downtown Detroit Union Depot. Iconic trains including "The Wolverine", and "Motor City Special" entered and departed from Michigan Central while downtown "The Ambassador" and "Red Arrow" called the Union Station home.

During World War II the majority of Detroit's soldiers, sailors and airmen utilized one or the other depots en route to military destinations across the country. The echo of loudspeakers reverberated throughout the cavernous waiting rooms announcing departures and arrivals - "Arriving Track 8 -The Twilight Limited, Departing Track 4 -The Wabash Cannonball" as servicemen and loved ones embraced and bid tearful farewells. At the end of hostilities they traveled home and departed and embarked through these same terminals. Most walked out to a joyous family reunion - some were met by my Dad.

The next of kin of a "Fallen Hero" were presented with four options in relation to a final resting place.

1. To be interred at a Permanent American Military Cemetery overseas.

2. To be returned to the United States or any possession or territory thereof for interment by next of kin in a private cemetery.

3. To be returned (insert foreign country) for interment by next of kin.

4. To be returned to the United States for final interment in a National Cemetery.

The George Van Kula Funeral Home had the distinct honor and privilege of handling the final arrangements for twelve World War II departed warriors.

From the time of death to the ultimate hometown arrival, proper identification of the deceased remained a top priority. Graves Registration Units scoured the battlefields of Europe and the Pacific attempting to ensure that all remains were accurately identified and

given a proper burial. Sadly to say this was not always possible –
graves of "UNKNOWNS" dot the landscape of European and
Pacific military cemeteries. Depending on the place of death, the
remains once identified were interred in a temporary cemetery and
later transferred to a permanent military cemetery.

The "Repatriation Program" was a massive military operation
involving thousands of personnel throughout the world. Initial
groundwork began in 1945 but it wasn't until 1947 that the first
shipment of remains arrived back in the United States. On October
10, 1947 The United States Army transport ship, "HONDA
KNOT" passed under the Golden Gate Bridge into San Francisco
Bay with 3,012 flag draped caskets from the Pacific Theater of
war. Sixteen days later, on October 26, 1947 the "JOSEPH V.
CONNOLLY" sailed into Pier 61 in the New York Harbor with
6,248 casketed remains from the European Theater. Thus began
the return of over 233,000 or 56% of those killed in action to the
United States for burial. Of the 407,000 plus United States combat
deaths, Michigan ranked 7th with 12,885.

The sight that parents or spouses and family members feared
most were the appearance of military personnel on their front porch.
This signified one of two things – their son or husband was killed
or missing in action. With the cessation of hostilities the families
of those killed in action were presented with options in regards to
a final burial site. If they chose to have the remains returned for
interment in the United States, they contacted their funeral director
of choice who was contacted by the government and notified of
the date and place of arrival of the body. The funeral director then
informed the family and final funeral arrangements were initiated.
After years of patient and mournful apprehension the family
prepared to write the final chapter.

Upon arrival at either the New York or San Francisco port of embarkation the remains were shipped by train to one of the 15 transfer points strategically located throughout the United States. The railroad transport point for Michigan from the New York embarkation port was Columbus, Ohio, from San Francisco it was Chicago, Illinois. From Columbus or Chicago the casket was transferred to a Detroit bound train. Accompanying the remains was a military escort of the same branch of service and of equal or higher rank of the deceased. The escort remained with the body from the placement on the train at the distribution center to the final burial at the hometown cemetery.

On a few occasions I accompanied Dad to the Detroit train station and witnessed the transfer from the train to the hearse. The casket was enclosed in a wooden shipping case and was given priority status in the railroad's loading and unloading procedure. Travelers passing through the marbled arches of the terminal were unaware and oblivious to the black hearse lurking in the shadows of the baggage area.

Depending on the wishes of the family the remains laid in state at the family residence or at the funeral home where an honor guard was usually posted by a local chapter of the American Legion or Veterans of Foreign Wars. The fallen serviceman was entitled to full military burial honors which included a bugler, pall bearers and an honor guard rifle squad for the rendering of a three volley salute. These "burial units" consisted of "short timers" who were anxiously awaiting their military discharge and were stationed locally at Fort Wayne in Detroit or Selfridge Field in Mt. Clemens. In the event these personnel were unavailable an honor squad was usually available through the American Legion or VFW.

On one occasion circa 1948 Dad contacted Fort Wayne and requested an honor squad consisting of a bugler and rifle squad – the family provided the pallbearers. On the appointed morning the unit met Dad at St. Nicholas Church on East Grand Boulevard where Dad informed them that the church service would last approximately 90 minutes. As their services weren't needed until the final committal at the cemetery they were presented with two options: 1. wait at the church until the completion of the services or 2. locate a venue that would occupy 90 minutes of their time. They opted for number 2 – a local tavern a few blocks from the church.

Unfortunately at the completion of the church services and as mourners were entering their vehicles for the journey to the cemetery the soldiers were AWOL. Dad quickly dispatched his assistant down to the Joseph Campau beer garden to retrieve the crew with the bugle and rifles. Fortunately they rejoined the cortege in time and discharged their duties at the cemetery – although I'm not sure of the timing of their rifle volley.

One fact that I am extremely proud to mention is that during the 50 year history of The Van Kula Funeral Home every effort was made to obtain the services of a bugler for a veteran's funeral. We even had a father and son team on call for the purpose of rendering taps at the cemetery. It was the least we could have done for the sacrifices they made for our freedom.

During World War II many restrictions were placed on a multitude of manufacturing operations including caskets and burial vaults. Steel or metal caskets were no longer permitted to be produced. Wooden caskets and or cloth covered wooden caskets would have to suffice for the duration. One burial vault company converted from making vaults to making 100 lb. bombs.

Post 49 Namesake Buried

Honór guard of the John A. Cougler Post 49 carry the remains of their post namesake from the Resurrection church after a solemn high requiem mass was read. A post honor guard maintained a 48 hour vigil as the body laid in state. Pfc. Cougler was killed in Australia early in 1942, one of the first Detroit draftees to die in the service of his country.

—AMVET Photo by John Sternicki

Dad conducting the funeral of PFC John A. Cougler - March 6, 1948

Casketed remains from European Theater
respectfully unloaded at Pier 61, New York Harbor - 1948

Fort Street Union Depot Wabash Cannonball

Copyright 1945 Lone Ranger Inc.   A··   "Lone Ranger Astride Hi Yo Silver"   Permission granted for Newspaper and Magazine reproduction.

Brace Beemer (The Lone Ranger) and
Silver Paint Creek Acres Ranch Oxford, Michigan

CHAPTER SEVEN

THE 1950'S

With the advent of my educational career in the fall of 1948 about to commence, my position with the firm was of a limited nature – an afternoon of kindergarten was on the horizon. SS. Cyril and Methodius Slovak Catholic Church and accompanying High School and Grade School were located directly across the street from the funeral home/residence. This geographic fact was often brought to my attention many times as being advantageous – other than the fact that the walk to school being of a short duration, I could think of no other.

Even though I had entered the academic world I still managed on occasion to accompany Dad on a few of his travel excursions - death certificate filing trips downtown, chasing down a doctor and one in particular that created havoc with my young mind. Staffing St. Cyril School were the Dominican Sisters of Oxford, Michigan. A very dedicated community of religious women who spent the better part of 13 years attempting to educate me – the key word being attempting. At the age of five what they did accomplish was to instill in me a sense of fear. Outfitted in their black and white habits and their oversized rosary beads dangling at their side, they projected an authoritarian presence of prodigious proportions. By a single phone call to your parents they could make life very difficult.

For all of their numerous positive attributes they remained vulnerable in one human endeavor – they couldn't drive. Even if they could they didn't have a car. Enter George Van Kula Sr., owner and operator of the local funeral home, owner and operator of a four door Cadillac and also due to the nature of his profession often available for favors at convenient times of day or night. To further advance their academic credentials the good Sisters were enrolled in various evening courses at two of Detroit's citadels of higher learning – The University of Detroit and Wayne State University. It would be safe to assume that Drivers Training was not listed on any of their class schedules.

Falling under the category of public relations or just plain "Mr. Nice Guy" Dad began and spawned a chauffeuring career that encompassed many years. In addition to maintaining and operating a funeral home, sharing in the raising of six children, being an active member and participant in an assortment of civic, fraternal, business and religious organizations Dad and I registered many hours ferrying nuns from convent to campus and back. To be perfectly honest I wasn't all that ecstatic confronting them in a daily classroom environment, let alone as passengers in the family car. On these trips as I sat motionless in the front seat I was hoping against hope that one of them wouldn't blurt out one of my many transgressions that might have occurred earlier in the school day. Hair shirts of the religious fanatics held no sway on this kid – I sweated out enough penance in those car trips of the past to get me out of two trips to hell.

Eventually two events transpired in the mid 1950's that eliminated the need for the Van Kula taxi service – Sister Bertrand acquiring a Michigan Driver's License and the acquisition of a "NUNMOBILE" – a 1955 Plymouth station wagon. Its arrival at the convent was acknowledged with a chorus of smiling faces – none more revealing than the one on the face of the local funeral director.

With the dawn of the 1950's life on St. Cyril Avenue was good – as a matter of fact it was pretty good throughout the country as the post war economy continued to grow. Detroit's population peaked at 1.86 million people in 1950 – it would never get any higher. The neighborhood auto and manufacturing plants were operating at close to full capacity, people got dressed up to go downtown shopping or to take in a movie and streetcars were still motoring along ten major thoroughfares and Detroit Edison was still exchanging light bulbs for free. SS. Cyril & Methodius Catholic Church listed over 1500 families as members and the high school and grade school had an enrollment of over 800 students. The Red Wings were packing them in the "Old Red Barn" (Olympia Stadium) and in the process won four Stanley Cups during the 1950's. The football Lions managed to capture three (3) national championships (not a typo) in the decade. The "Tigers" were struggling over at Briggs Stadium on the corner of Michigan and Trumbull and the "Pistons" still played basketball in Fort Wayne, Indiana until 1957. In 1953 over at the WXYZ TV studios in the Maccabees Building on Woodward Avenue Soupy Sales invited kids to join him for "LUNCH WITH SOUPY".

True Detroiters are cognizant of the fact that in reality there exist two Detroit's – East Side and West Side. Woodward Avenue which runs north and south from the Detroit Riverfront to the city limits at 8 mile road geographically bisects the city. Occupants and residents of the east side rarely ventured west of Woodward and west siders generally didn't stray east. Even the Mafia back in the day followed tradition and formed a west side gang and an east side gang.

Going out to dinner was still a major and infrequent social event for most families. On those special occasions we'd pile into the Cadillac and head out to Sid's on East Warren or Downtown to the Book Cadillac. My favorite was The Stockholm on East Jefferson and Rivard (A Swedish smorgasbord that in 1963 Hugh Hefner transformed into a smorgasbord of booze, breasts and bunnies – The Detroit Playboy Club) - liked it even better then.

Kitty corner to the funeral home old man Geras still sold penny candy for a penny in his grocery store and Marion Sweet Shop down on Van Dyke Avenue (between Marcus and Marion) was my go to place for ice cream treats and the latest in new comic book adventures. But when finances allowed I would trek five blocks south on Van Dyke for the ultimate and preeminent destination for neighborhood ten year olds – "LAWRENCE'S TOY STORE". Lawrence's was a virtual cornucopia of toys and other neat stuff – one entire wall contained hundreds of previously read comic books. On a Saturday afternoon it wasn't uncommon to encounter six to eight literary giants sprawled out on the floor checking out the latest adventures of "Superman", "Batman" or "Archie and Jughead". It was sort of a Christian Science Reading Room for comic book junkies. In retrospect I believe the toy racket may have just been a sideline as Lawrence spent an inordinate amount of time conversing on the phone. I always assumed he had a lot of friends. But the "Big Four" (Detroit's no nonsense detective squad) who made periodic visits assumed otherwise. Rumors circulated that it had something to do with horses and betting. Be that as it may, Lawrence and his store remain one of my favorite childhood recollections. More than once he cut me a deal when I came up a nickel or dime short on my purchase of some really neat stuff that I couldn't live without.

For the most part neighbors were still neighborly, front doors went unlocked and weather permitting front porches became social magnets. Many summer days and evenings the front porches of Marcus Street provided the setting for board games, baseball card trading or just plain BS sessions. Of course as a kid in the early 50's you realized early on that not all neighborhood kids shared your outlook on life, liberty and the pursuit of happiness - there were certain streets and locations you avoided whenever possible. The area possessed its share of bad actors – mainly a few bullies whose claim to fame was that they were bigger than you and a lot less intelligent. Of course my physical physique at the time would be classified in the lightweight category. I was the proverbial 90lb. weakling in the Charles Atlas comic book ads that got sand kicked in his face- I never signed up for the course. I can relate to "Christmas Stories'" Ralphie and his nemesis Scut Farkus.

Alley: A narrow street or passageway between or behind city buildings or homes. A liberal portion of my childhood days evolved in or around the alley. It was definitely a lot safer to play in than the street - especially Marcus Street. Shift change at the nearby Plymouth Lynch Road Assembly Plant turned the surrounding streets into avenues of vehicular mayhem as autoworkers raced to and from the plant – raced being the operative verb. Shift change was not an opportune moment to cross or play in the street. The alley was our alternative playground to Lodge Park. I feel sorry for the youth of today domiciled in their tree lined, master planned, alley-less communities of suburbia. They will never share or experience the joys and disappointments of alley camaraderie. No alleys – how un-American. You place your garbage in front of your house for pickup – how gross! You expanded your vocabulary in the alley with words that the nuns would never teach. Your initial experience with tobacco usually took place in the alley corridor. You played in the alley: baseball, tennis ball hockey, kick the can, hide and seek, tag. Long live the alley!

Some Detroit alleys were paved, ours wasn't. This transgression on the part of the city fathers diminished its usefulness following a thunderstorm. Throughout the years, "Road Apples" became another obstacle to contend with in our recreational pursuits in the alley. In Detroit during the 1940's and 50's a group of individuals who plied their trade of junk collecting via the alleyways were referred to as "Sheeny Men". The nameless gentleman who usually patrolled our alley was friendly and was a fundamental part of the neighborhood along with the mailman and milkman. He even gave us rides on the wagon – for free. I can vividly recall when Dad utilized his services by having him cart out and dispose of a number of cast iron radiators from the basement of the funeral home. Dad displayed his appreciation with a few shots of Canadian Club. His horse was another matter. For some reason known only to God and the horse, the nag would invariably deposit a load of "Road Apples" directly behind our garage. You never went barefoot in the alley more than once.

Lodge Park or Georgia Park – take your pick – it answered to both – encompassed one city block and was the recreational epicenter of the neighborhood. Fronting the property on St. Cyril Avenue was The John T. Burroughs Junior High School. Perhaps its most famous or infamous alumnus was Robert Vesco who lived on Edgewood Street and is referred to as the "undisputed king of the fugitive financiers". He was charged with embezzling 220 million dollars and spent his life on the run. Another neighborhood kid makes good.

Two baseball diamonds, two softball diamonds, football field, clay tennis courts, wading pool, swings, sandbox, playground and maintenance building made up the physical layout of Lodge Park. During the winter months an ice pond was constructed by bulldozing mounds of dirt and filling the enclosure with water.

Penguins would have found it difficult to walk on the Lodge Park ice- humans found it almost impossible to skate on. During the summer months a park director appeared on the scene to oversee and coordinate activities. He passed out sporting equipment, organized the baseball league and a multitude of other tasks designed to keep the neighborhood urchins entertained and occupied.

What was unique in that era of the 1950's was the absence of adult and parental involvement. Dads were busy working and moms were busy momming. We organized our own baseball teams and attempted to obtain a sponsor for a hat and uniform jersey – sometimes we were successful. A new bat existed only on the racks of Eastside Sports – the local sporting goods outlet. We considered ourselves lucky if we had at least one nail-less bat. Most were hand me downs that were usually cracked or broken – getting them back to playing condition required a few nails and a few strands of black electrical tape. Practice balls hadn't seen a cowhide cover on them in months and most resembled ostrich eggs with their layers of white adhesive tape. We stacked the deck with the best neighborhood players in our age bracket to form the "Lodge Park Panthers". We won the park championship five years in a row.

One of the park's more infamous events occurred one summer evening in the 1950's. The City of Detroit decided that the neighborhood was ripe for some culture and scheduled an evening band concert. The Detroit Concert Band was formed from among the many talented Detroit musicians and performed summer concerts at various parks throughout the city. Parks and Recreation worker descended en- masse and transformed the tennis courts into a concert venue complete with stage, speakers, lighting and benches. As early evening began to fade into night the local populace began to arrive and by the time the maestro dropped the baton it was SRO. My mother, brother and I were seated

73

approximately 15 rows back from the stage. Outside the tennis courts and directly behind the stage was the maintenance building containing the restrooms and affectionately known to the kids on the block as "the shithouse".

Lurking on the roof of the building was an assortment of neighborhood delinquents. I'm sure these were the older elements of "punkdom" more than likely members of the Harper-Van Dyke gang. It all began midway through the first half of the program – rocks came raining down from the roof landing in the brass section followed by a barrage of fireworks and cherry bombs targeting the stage. The concert was over almost before it began. The concertmaster, on the verge of a coronary informed the crowd that he would never return to Lodge Park – he never did.

Once the Saturday chores were completed and financial remunerations were negotiated it was time to head south on Van Dyke to the movies. Cinematic choices were usually predetermined during a Friday recess with the boys. Movie houses of choice were The Eastown or The Van Dyke. The Eastown being the larger and more majestic generally presented first run flicks while "B" movies filled the screen of The Van Dyke. To mention that The Van Dyke was less majestic than The Eastown would be an understatement – what The Van Dyke lacked in class it made up for in the presence of holes in the screen and roof not to mention the mice that sauntered across the stage. But the price was right.

Most often our hard earned allowance filled the coffers of The Eastown. Saturday matinees consisted of serials, cartoons, a first run feature and an occasional appearance of The Duncan Yo-Yo Champion. Matinee lines usually snaked their way down from the Harper Avenue entrance around the corner and down Maxwell Street. After the show the Duncan rep, resplendent in his championship sweater vest put on an exhibition of the latest in yo-yo wizardry. It always ended with his pitch to buy a Duncan yo-yo.

Following the afternoon's festivities the eleven block homeward trek might include stops at one of the local dime stores, Lawrence's Toy Store or if you were frugal enough in your spending a burger and orange pop at The White Tower around the corner from The Eastown.

I was still trying the patience of the nuns as they continued to oversee and monitor my educational endeavors. I found it most gratifying to make it out of kindergarten being able to color within the lines. As I progressed through the ranks of St. Cyril grade school, my fledging career in funeral service was of a limited nature. Not unlike thousands of others who grew up in the confines of a family run business I joined my siblings in after school chores, weekend chores and summer vacation chores whenever the need arose. We possessed no prior knowledge of when Dad would be summoned to direct a funeral or the length of time the chapel would be occupied. We stood fast in the Boy Scout tradition of "Being Prepared".

Located in the lower level of the Sears Roebuck store on Gratiot and Van Dyke was the vacuum cleaner department. Every time I would pass by a salesman was holding court demonstrating the wonders of the latest Hoover. He would sprinkle glitter on a section of carpet and vacuum it up with the greatest of ease. No matter how many miles he put on that machine in a week he had nothing on this kid when I navigated the chapel carpet with my Hoover.

Highlighting the main entrance of the funeral home were two custom designed leaded beveled glass doors. Inside the foyer two leaded glass French doors enhanced the entry way into the chapel and office area. All four doors were masterpieces of beauty and charm and for me it was a love hate relationship. In the pre Windex days I was forced to use a product called "Glass Wax" which when applied dried to a powdery film. It was definitely a laborious task to remove the residue from the corners and edges of the leaded glass. Come to think of it after all these years in was a giant pain in the ass and it was made even more so as I witnessed through the hazy residue my buddies, gloves and bats in hand, heading for Lodge Park and a game of baseball.

One of the intrinsic benefits of surviving a Michigan winter was the eventual onset of spring: Mother Nature awakening the dormant plant life, "Opening Day", bikes being extracted from winter storage, the academic year approaching the home stretch and the Van Kula Family pilgrimage to the local sod farm. Snow and ice have never been my favorite byproducts of a Michigan winter. Individuals who extoll the beauty and majesty of a glistening, white mantle of fresh fallen snow either live in Arizona or own a ski resort in Northern Michigan. By the end of March chances are that the glistening white mantle has transformed into a curbside blanket of dingy, grimy, black mountainous frozen slush. My theory on snow, unfortunately not shared by my dad, was that God put it there and in time will eventually remove it.

By virtue of the funeral home's geographic corner location complete with traffic signal, we acquired more than our fair share of over the curb rock salt infested snow plow residue – residue whose salinity index was probably greater than that of The Dead Sea. Not only did rock salt trigger cancerous auto body rust and corrosion, it also killed grass. Thus every spring we headed down to the corner of Van Dyke and Roland Avenues to the local renter, hitched up a trailer and motored north to one of Macomb County's sod farms. It became a springtime tradition. Just as the President tossed out the first ball to signify the opening of baseball season, my Dad threw out a roll of fresh green Macomb County sod to signify the opening of grass cutting season.

One particular spring I attempted to persuade Dad to forego the sod and in its place erect bleachers. During daylight hours St. Cyril Avenue was a peaceful, residential, tree-lined thoroughfare. Nights it became synonymous with the quarter mile straightaway at The Detroit Dragway. 9074 St. Cyril was strategically located halfway between the two major curves on the avenue. Squealing tires, full throttled engines, screeching brakes, breaking glass, crunching metal were frequent sounds that shattered the air on many a night on my time spent on St. Cyril Avenue.

Once the sod found its proper place around the periphery of the building it was time to initiate phase two – flowers. A Saturday morning trip to Detroit's famed Eastern Market was in order to garner flowers to grace the concrete flower pots and window box. This trip wasn't without benefits – a visit to The Gratiot Central Market for a corned beef sandwich and a bottle of Orange Crush.

At the conclusion of the spring planting season plans were set in motion to test the artistic skills of the family. Surrounding the porches was an intricate wrought iron railing that necessitated a yearly paint job. In addition there were numerous awning and canopy support pipes that yearned for a spring coat of oil based green paint. Throw in some 3-4 dozen metal flower stands for good measure and the lineup was complete. Out came the steel wool to render the rust areas invisible and ensure that all surfaces were brush ready. Dad had one hard and fast rule – no paint on the brickwork, concrete porch surface or sidewalk. He even graciously supplied a bountiful supply of cardboard to act as a surface shield in the event of a mishap. It didn't take me long to realize that an oil based green paint and concrete combination didn't set too well with the old man. As careful as one could be, and how careful is a ten or twelve year old, the inevitable occurred and out came the wire brush.

After I retired from the outside painting detail, my younger brother, David, inherited the task and if memory serves me correctly he held the position for only one season. David was ensconced in the garage, double doors open applying the requisite green paint to the collection of flower stands. In attendance was a smattering of his neighborhood disciples. Realizing that there was speed in numbers he passed out brushes to those assembled and sat back to reflect on his astuteness. Unfortunately he failed to mention Dad's "no paint on the concrete" edict to his minions. Within a short period of time Dad drove up, parked the car and approached the garage with his Slovak blood pressure approaching dangerous levels. Before his eyes the driveway was a canvas of green droplets that would have made Andy Warhol proud. What transpired next was not pretty – I do recollect David wearing out some wire brushes in an attempt to bring the driveway and sidewalk back to its former glory.

In addition to possessing a reputation as a pseudo drag strip, St. Cyril Avenue was often referred to as "The Avenue of Funeral Processions". Conveniently located between the funeral homes and churches of the Detroit's lower eastside and the cemeteries of the upper eastside, it functioned as a strategic short cut for funeral processions. It wasn't uncommon on some Saturdays to have a dozen or more funeral processions passing by on their journey to Forest Lawn or Mt. Olivet Cemeteries.

Saturday morning's arrival in the old neighborhood was heralded by a conglomeration of sights, sounds and smells: the monotonous clanking of oil-less wheels of manual lawn mowers, an increase in pedestrian and vehicular traffic, occasionally the sounds of a polka band performing on the porch of the bride as she prepared for her wedding, palatable aromas of freshly baked bread and paczki emanating from the St. Cyril Bakery and eventually the high pitched sound of a police siren.

The siren was mounted on a Harley Davison motorcycle and ridden by a member of The Detroit Police Department – sometimes there were two or three. It was a dead giveaway (pun intended) of an approaching funeral procession. If I was a betting man, and I am, my money would wager that the approaching cortege was Italian in nature. Of course it would be an unfair bet – Italian funeral processions always had police escorts – even one car Italian funerals. Black funeral processions were distinctive in nature and that characteristic that separated them from others was speed. For whatever reason due to the velocity of the hearse and ensuing motorcade I was under the impression they were in a hurry to reach the cemetery.

The mysteries of my Father's profession launched a constant dialogue of curiosity among my friends and classmates. Inquiries concerning death, embalming, dead bodies and our families' position on the economic ladder were continually put forth. "You're rich cause your Dad drives a big Cadillac and you live in a big house" was an often repeated phrase of my youth. Middle class maybe, but if we were rich the folks did one hell of a job hiding it from us. Dad's car of choice was a no-brainer – it was dependable and spacious. It served its purpose transporting clergy, altar boys and bereaved families. Ranking near the top of the interrogation scale was the time honored and venerable query – "How do they embalm a body?" Now shooting that question to a ten year old was paramount to asking a cardiologist's kid how his dad performed open heart surgery. I didn't have the foggiest notion and to be perfectly honest at that age I really didn't care.

If embalming ranked number one on the query list, "What do they do with the blood?" was number two. Now this one I knew – it went down the drain -we had a sewer connection in the garage. That answer would have been too tame for the neighborhood urchins therefore I told them we bottled it and sold it to the Russians. Some may have even believed it. I probably received more requests to witness an embalming procedure than Augusta National gets for Masters' tickets. Of course this was a totally impossible petition to honor but that didn't stop a lifetime of requests.

The morgue was situated on the south end of the multi-car garage and contained two windows. One was permanently sealed in with an exhaust fan and the other was a frosted privacy window. At times the privacy window would be opened a few inches to permit a flow of fresh air. Outside and alongside the south wall of the morgue was a walkway and fence. There were a few occasions when the more daring of the local hellions climbed the fence, leaned over and attempted a sneak preview through the narrow opening of the privacy window. It was a futile attempt due to the angle of the opening. All that was visible was a portion of the opposite wall and totally impossible to observe any of the embalming procedure. Ultimately their presence was discovered by either Dad or the embalmer and challenged in a most unpleasant manner. If "Peeping Tommery" was their objective I'm sure there were other neighborhood windows that would have offered a more enticing target than the portholes of the local funeral home morgue. But these were the kids of "My Neighborhood" and they would have been quite capable of ruffling the cardigans of Mr. Rogers – He would have had to make some major adjustments if he lived on Marcus Street.

For many years a familiar and endearing gentleman traversed the streets and sidewalks of the city blocks surrounding the corner of St. Cyril and Marcus – "Pete the Mailman". Pete was a black man servicing an all-white eastside Detroit neighborhood. He was friendly, outgoing and possessed an infectious smile and personality. He knew all the neighborhood urchins by their first name and during the summer months he was one of the most popular, if not the most popular letter carrier in the employ of the Post Office. If by chance you happened to be in the area of St. Cyril and Marcus at the same time as Pete you were more than likely the beneficiary of a summertime treat. Pete would enter either old man Geras' market or "Mary's" Kowalski store and emerge with popsicles for all his tag-alongs. I have no idea what a postman's salary was in the 1950's but I'm sure there was no significant ice cream allowance. But that's how Pete rolled. As the Christmas Holidays approached Dad would show his appreciation by presenting him with a couple of bottles of high end hooch and a box of Sanders candy. I can remember a few miserable Michigan snow blown mornings as he was delivering our mail, when Dad would greet him at the door, invite him in and get his blood circulating with a couple of shots of Canadian Club. Pete was a true gentlemen and a fond memory of my childhood.

Besides the last day of school and perhaps Christmas Day the most anticipated event in the neighborhood of my youth was Halloween. As the magical day arrived the first order of business was the filling of the legendary Van Kula Halloween bags. Returning home from a hard day of book learning, me and the siblings found the dining room table loaded with an assortment of boxed confectionery delights, Halloween bags and the stapler. The mission: fill 200-250 bags for the evening's trick or treaters. Over the years the funeral home became one of the favorite stops for the neighborhood goblins.

With the advent of dusk and the wolfing down of an early dinner it was time to meet up with the guys and attack the streets: Marcus, Kern, Roland, Merkel, St. Cyril were first on the list.

Then it was time to head home, drop off the bulging pillowcase, pick up another and head south to Georgia, Erbie, Genoa and Maywood. By then it was time for the "Piece de resistance" - the bright lights of Van Dyke Avenue and the neighborhood beer gardens – "Jo-Yorks", "Tony's Bar", "I & J Bar", "Grasshopper Bar" to name a few. This was "cash country" – no Tootsie Rolls, Necco Wafers of Root Beer Barrels here – nickels and dimes were on the menu – dispensed by patrons and management. Then the posse headed for home to examine, explore and indulge in the plethora of the night's treasures. One of the advantages of attending Catholic school manifested itself the day after Halloween – All Saints Day – A holy day of obligation which transcended into no school.

One memorable Halloween night remains with me after six decades. Normally by 9 P.M. the calls of "Help the Poor" were fading out and the begging action was dwindling down. If there were any stragglers they were normally the bigger kids – teen agers. I was sitting inside the front door of the funeral home on the vestibule steps when four black teenage boys stopped on the sidewalk in front of the funeral home. A heated debate ensued among them. Three of them wanted to approach the front door, while the fourth member of the group let it be known to one and all "I ain't going to no funeral home -- they got dead bodies in there". The three that approached the front door didn't seem too thrilled to be on the funeral home porch either, but they accepted the bags of candy with gratitude. I couldn't resist. I hollered down to their friend on the sidewalk, "Do you want to come in and see some dead bodies?" He never answered. Of course by the fact that he was bolting down St. Cyril faster than a speeding bullet led me to believe he wasn't interested. I don't think he came back the next year.

St. Cyril's grade school curriculum of the 1950's included Religion, Spelling, Arithmetic, Art, Music, English, Geography,

Health, Handwriting (Cursive) and Reading. One subject conspicuously absent from the list is Slovak. It is hard to believe that the only Slovak Catholic High School and Grade School in the City of Detroit would not teach the Slovak language. One feeble excuse put forth many years ago was the reason for this faux pas was that due to the recent influx of Slovak immigrants to the church and school they wanted everyone to become "Americanized" and put their past and culture behind them.

Academic subjects aside, the most important and relevant grade on that report card in the opinion of George and Anne Van Kula began with a "C" – Courtesy! A mark of "A" was expected, a "B" was tolerated, a "C" was cause for alarm, a "D" created parental havoc and God forbid a "U" was cause for you to phone the nearest foreign legion recruiter. Although I must say I never had to place that call I kept the number handy just in case. To make the honor roll an "A" or "B" was required in the courtesy department – I can remember more than a few instances where a "C" deprived me of academic honors. It was times like these you hoped that you could circumvent the attention of the old man and deal with the soft touch – Mom. Or I could have adopted my older sister's method of report card signing – forgery. She wouldn't have made the grade as a counterfeiter – she got nailed on the first try.

"CLEANLINESS IS NEXT TO GODLINESS" could have been the official proverb for SS. Cyril & Methodius School if they had one. It wasn't posted on the curriculum or listed on the report card but it was an integral element of the school agenda – cleaning. Due to the size and magnitude of the physical structure it proved to be a demanding task for the two custodians to continually maintain a high standard of performance. Christmas, Easter and the termination of classes in June were earmarked as major cleaning projects – entailing the washing of countless windows, the scrubbing and waxing of hundreds of square feet of church, classroom and hallway floors – a monumental task for two middle aged men. How could a labor pool of over 800 students be accessed to provide assistance? The nuns were street wise enough to know the futility of requesting volunteers – enter the demerit system. Infractions ranged from tardiness, talking in class or church, chewing gum, throwing snowballs, absence of homework or smoking in the john. Punishment was doled out in doses of 40 minute after school detention periods.

Certain repeat offenders had their parents convinced that the correct dismissal time was 40 minutes later than it actually was. Doing time sometimes entailed writing penance, a cleaning detail or the dreaded request of a parental visit. On the surface the demerit system was a noble and time honored procedure for the maintenance of law and order in a parochial school of the 1950's. The issuance of demerits rose to astronomical proportions preceding the Christmas, Easter and summer vacation periods. With a flick of the "BIC" the nuns filled the labor pool.

As the dog days of the Michigan summer approached Labor Day anticipation of the pending school year became the topic of front porch conversation on Marcus Street. In the final week of August teacher and room assignments were posted on the front doors of SS. Cyril & Methodius School. Trepidation and apprehension abounded as you approached the listings that would determine your fate for the impending academic year. Among the student body nuns weren't ranked by their academic credentials but by their personality and classroom demeanor. Everyone knew who the few hardliners were and hoped against hope their name wouldn't appear on their room assignment. Then there were the instances when Oxford sent out a rookie – a first timer to the hallowed halls of St.Cyril – an unknown. Of course no one had a say in the matter but it made for interesting dialogue and you accepted the hand or the nun you were dealt.

A disciplinary tool in vogue at the time among the Dominicans was either the 18" wooden ruler or the 36" wooden yard stick. The 18 incher was the weapon of choice in the war on snowball throwing. A fresh morning snowfall provided the impetus for the lunchtime entertainment – throwing snowballs: At each other, girls, passing cars, the school building, smaller-kids – the targets were incidental. Of course these actions were totally and irrevocably against school policy. I believe if Moses ever got a number 11 it would read "Thou shall not throw snowballs!" Nothing brought the wrath of nunnery down on your head more quickly than participating in the dastardly act of throwing a God made snowball. Retribution was swift, merciless and painful.

Returning to your classroom seat after lunch you envisioned the impending doom. Depending on the magnitude and fallout of the outdoor snowball activity a visit from the principal herself might be warranted. With her arrival you knew this was some serious stuff. Whoever was wielding the 18 incher would ultimately pose a simple question – "Who was throwing snowballs?" As far as I can remember no one ever answered in the affirmative. Actually they didn't have to – your hands betrayed you. They were cold, wet and turning blue. Of course you could have avoided the consequences and perhaps gotten away with it by simply wearing gloves – but you were cool – guys never wore gloves. Thus you became a victim of the snowball wars.

You sat upright gritting your teeth, palms down on the top of your desk as the wooden ruler came slamming down on your knuckles. If you were lucky you only got one swat per hand. Can you imagine in today's world where this would end up? The ACLU would be going spastic, "Mothers Against Nun Violence" would be forming MANV chapters throughout the country and lawyers would be lined up and down St. Cyril Avenue.

One of the dear sisters exhibited a preference for the 36" wooden yard stick – I think she bought them by the gross. She preferred the two handed grip and her swing and follow through would have made Mantle proud. Her target of choice was usually across your back and more often than not this resulted in the shattering of the yard stick.

Back in the day a "Snow Day" was exactly what the phrase implied – a day it was snowing. In today's wussified society a minor dusting of flakes usually results in a massive closure of educational facilities. There were days when blizzard conditions prevailed and the doors to St. Cyril School remained open for all to enter. One weather- related episode occurred during a frigid Michigan winter morning that after time I find quite humorous – as a matter of fact I found it quite humorous when it occurred. The boiler quit boiling – the massive building was devoid of heat. You could see your breath. Thoughts of an early dismissal and a day off danced in our heads. Suddenly the PA system came alive and reverberated with the Principal's command, "Attention classes, attention please!" Student smiles widened as we anticipated the impending day of academic freedom. She continued, "Everyone go to your lockers and get your hats, gloves and jackets and return to your classroom." Are you kidding me? Have you ever attempted to write cursive with a gloved hand? Snow Days – Don't mess with Mother Nature or the Oxford Dominicans.

This was the 1950's and rebellious youth were being categorized as "Juvenile Delinquents". Among the student body of St. Cyril at the time I'm sure there were a few individuals that fell into that category. Of course they were weeded out as soon as their unconventional behavior manifested itself in a classroom environment. One particular eighth grade moment has remained with me through the passage of time. The soon to be ex-student became involved in a shouting match which soon escalated into a shoving match with Sister "No Nonsense". The fracas was terminated when the nun tossed the culprit into the decorated classroom Christmas tree. Dripping with tinsel and garland the miscreant was unceremoniously escorted out the front door to continue his education at a public school.

The newspaper article is yellowed with age but the headline is as vibrant as the day it was published on March 16, 1954 in "The Detroit Times" – "MYSTERY PRANKS" – "COUPLE RECEIVES A FLOOD OF UNORDERED DISORDER". The articles first sentence: "Somebody with a highly fertile imagination and a deeply rooted grudge against George and Anne Van Kula is rapidly driving them to the border of hysteria." After all these years I would like to post an addendum: "Some jerk with a warped sense of humor and too much time on his hands".

It began with a house call from a local veterinarian inquiring about our sick dog. We didn't have a dog and we never called the vet. The doggie doctor was followed by a parade of delivery men and women transporting everything from juke boxes, typewriters, flowers, BBQ chickens, ice cream and a multitude of other unordered items. Tow trucks arrived along with TV repairmen and loaded coal trucks. We were inundated with merchandise and deliveries over a four day period. Not content with creating havoc with the inhabitants of 9074 St. Cyril, not to mention the local merchants, the brainless prankster took it one step further – he placed ads in Detroit's weekend newspapers - one stating that we had an upper flat for rent (cheap) and the other for a handyman (good wages). Phone calls, job seekers and flat seekers pestered the family throughout the weekend. What was even more disturbing is that we had a body in state in the funeral home at the time. The Detroit Police were contacted but their investigation drew blanks - the chaos eventually ceased but not before garnering the attention of Detroit's three daily newspapers and "Time Magazine". It definitely was publicity of an unwanted nature. As the years passed I eventually learned the identity of the neighborhood psycho but never his motive.

After all these years I'm still at a loss as to how I pulled off summer trips to Pennsylvania. Perhaps it was more of my parents wanting to get rid of me for an extended period of time rather than my enthusiastic petitions. Dad's brother and sisters still occupied the family residence on Clarendon Avenue down in Uniontown, Pennsylvania. In the 1950's trains were still a viable means of transportation and the two I travelled on were the Pennsylvania Railroad's "Red Arrow" and the Baltimore and Ohio's "Ambassador" – an experience I am thankful to have had before quality rail travel in the United States disappeared. Can't remember what specific events caused my excitement level to increase more in anticipation of my summer holiday – the solo train rides – weeks without brothers and sisters – no chores- being on my own – Pennsylvania?

As my aunts and uncle were all single and childless I was placed in a position of being somewhat "special", although not that special as they were all old school. Days were spent sleeping in, traipsing one mile down Morgantown Hill to downtown's Main Street to visit one of the three movie houses: The Penn, Manos or State, visiting the corner drug store for vanilla malts, riding bikes and catching fireflies with the family of girls next door. Riding bikes up and down the hills of Uniontown was an enormous high for this city boy. Riding bikes when a serious mechanical malfunction occurred quickly reduced the high to a low. As I was descending downhill on West Highland Avenue approaching my turn onto Clarendon Avenue, I applied pedal pressure for braking – the application didn't work – there were no brakes. "Houston we have a problem!" Gaining speed I jumped the curb on Clarendon and was headed for a 15 foot drop off into a neighbor's yard with the potential landing area – the top of an apple tree. Within inches of the drop off I bailed as the bike sailed on and landed on the tree. With scratches and bruises but no serious injuries I gathered myself up and headed out to gather forces to help retrieve the two- wheeler from the apple tree – "Don't land in the apple tree without anyone else but me".

The nighttime view from the second floor hallway window on Clarendon Avenue still remains vivid in my mind with the passage of time. Many were the nights I would sit and gaze out and witness the glowing and radiant bright orange and yellow flames rising to the heavens from the coke ovens still operating within the vicinity of the Uniontown of the 1950's. My Uncle John who spent a lifetime working the area ovens would inform me of the names and locations of the mining operations on the surrounding hillsides. Cousins still resided in Continental #2 – still do – and I would spend a portion of my lazy summer days in the patch town. The Company Store which opened in 1903 was still serving the residents of the patch town and my Aunt Elizabeth was still in its employ. Cousin Corky who was about my age and I would venture across the street from his house armed with BB guns and explore the remnants of the Continental #2 Coal and Mine Works which ceased operations in 1926. The mine was closed off and flooded but one area provided us with the opportunity to drop rocks down into the shaft and listen for the splash and accompanying echo from a hundred feet below. We traversed up and on and around the deteriorating coke ovens that were gradually being overgrown with vegetation, not giving any thought at the time of my Dad and Grandfather's presence on this very site 40 years prior. No I didn't shoot my eye out.

My railroad ticket from Detroit to Pittsburgh was always of the one way variety as Mom, Dad and siblings traveled to Uniontown every Labor Day weekend for the "Otpust". The "Otpust" was a pilgrimage to Our Lady of Perpetual Help that was held on the grounds of Mount St. Macrina. The estate was formerly known as "Oak Hill" the 1,000 acre manor of J.V. Thompson a Fayette County millionaire coal and coke baron who died penniless. In 1933 the property was acquired by the Sisters of St. Basil the Great and was renamed Mount St. Macrina and was the site of their motherhouse and a yearly pilgrimage of thanksgiving. In 1955 the "Otpust" with over 100,000 people in attendance featured television's Bishop Fulton J. Sheen who became the first Latin Rite Prelate to celebrate the Divine Liturgy of the Byzantine Rite in English. Dad and I had the honor of meeting Bishop Sheen in 1951 at the dedication of the Byzantine Rite Seminary in Pittsburgh, Pennsylvania.

Leaving the hills of southwestern Pennsylvania behind, I headed home with the family a little heavier, a little wiser and ready to approach another year of funeral home reality and educational objectives at St. Cyril School.

September not only heralded the beginning of a new academic year it also signaled the advent of the new model year – the moment for Detroit's introduction to the world of the latest automobile creations. It was the season of high drama and anticipation – bigger fins? more chrome?, increased horsepower? It was a time when cars were unique and you could differentiate one from the other. Auto plants across the neighborhood and city went to great lengths to tighten security. Canvas coverings draped the fences of the parking lots where the new assembly line arrivals were being temporarily stored. New car dealerships blacked out their showroom windows. Rotating searchlights set Detroit's sky aglow as the individual models made their debut at their respective dealerships. City-wide new model unveilings rivaled any "Tinseltown" premier. A portion of the route of our Sunday morning sojourn to St. Nicholas Church on East Grand Boulevard involved traveling on Dunn Road. Dunn Road ran north and south and paralleled the massive Dodge Main complex. New model time saw the street filled with the curious peeking through holes in the security canvas - we never stopped - Dad was a GM guy.

In the late 1940's the Dominican Sisters were outgrowing their convent on Van Dyke Avenue in the city of Warren and were on the hunt for larger facilities for their growing congregation.

Forty two miles north of St. Cyril Avenue in northern Oakland County lies the Village of Oxford. The hunt stopped there. They purchased a 160 acre estate and former dairy farm complete with three lakes on West Drahner Road.

Every May and October the Oxford property was the scene of a Sunday rosary pilgrimage of which the St. Cyril student body participated – attendance was mandatory. At the conclusion of the religious services we were allotted a few hours of free time to explore the estate. For this "city boy" this was something I looked forward to – traipsing about the estate and countryside in the midst of my two favorite seasons – Spring and Fall. Abutting the western boundary of the property was the 300 acre Paint Creek Ranch. Assembling the band of guys I was hanging with at the time we began our trek in the direction of the ranch with one determined purpose in mind – to visit "THE FIERY HORSE WITH THE SPEED OF LIGHT, THE GREAT HORSE SILVER!" Yes, that Silver! Paint

Creek Ranch was the home of Brace Beemer the radio voice of "The Lone Ranger" from 1941 until 1954.

In 1953 "The Lone Ranger" was being broadcast 3 times per week (Monday, Wednesday and Friday at 7:30 P.M.) on 249 stations across the United States to a cumulative audience of close to 15 million listeners per week. We were in luck in our quest for Silver – it was as if he was anticipating our arrival as we approached his barn. We fed him some apples, petted him, bid him farewell and headed back to the Detroit bound busses - Unfortunate that we never had the opportunity to meet Brace Beemer. According to the nuns he was a neighborly neighbor and a frequent visitor to the Motherhouse. I wonder if any of the good Sisters ever had the opportunity to ride Silver?

Home entertainment on St. Cyril was provided courtesy of our Philco Radio Console. As we turned the set on and tubes warmed up we eagerly awaited the exploits of "The Lone Ranger", "The Green Hornet", "Sgt. Preston of the Yukon" and a myriad of other dramatic offerings.

Whether the downstairs chapel was vacant or occupied dictated the volume setting. The above mentioned programs were created and produced at the studios of WXYZ Radio. They were originally broadcast from the Maccabees Building on Woodward near Wayne State University. In 1944 radio operations moved to the Mendelssohn Mansion located on Van Dyke and Iroquois Avenue. Both sites were approximately four miles from St. Cyril Avenue - So close and yet so far away. To fully appreciate and understand those sounds of the airwaves a vivid imagination was necessary. Today the faculty of imagination has been replaced by the microchip.

A black and white TV eventually supplanted the Philco in the corner of the living room. It now became possible to test your radio imagination to an image. Sometime in 1956 the image got the best of me – prior to this incident a bit of background is in order.

It was a spring time Saturday afternoon and my parents and siblings were to attend some long forgotten function for a few hours. I was to be left in charge. The downstairs chapel was unoccupied. My responsibilities were twofold: Answer the front door if a family arrived to make funeral arrangements, gather some pertinent information and contact Dad who would immediately return and take over. Secondly babysit the business phone (WA 1 4370).

I was anticipating a peaceful and solitary afternoon – no parents, no brothers or sisters. I had made the big time – I was in charge. Turning on the TV and channeling in the Tigers' game I sat back confident that no one would die that afternoon. I was wrong. I was about to take my first death call – many more would follow over the next 30 years. After securing the necessary vital information from the caller I informed him that Dad would contact him shortly. I called Dad and passed on the information.

Passing my initial test with high marks Dad felt confident enough in my abilities to present me with another challenge. Daytime phone duty was one thing, evening phone duty ranked a notch higher on the responsibility ladder – you had to stay awake. It was another long forgotten Saturday evening social function – in all probability a relative's wedding. After bidding the final visitor farewell and closing down the chapel Dad returned to the social activity. I remained behind – I was in charge again.

Securely ensconced in the upstairs living quarters I faced the next few hours with one objective in mind – stay awake. The chance of a walk in was extremely remote due to the late hour. Answering the business phone became priority number one -as in my initial "In Charge" experience the magical medium of television provided companionship. You might surmise correctly that a rational mind would not take this opportunity to view a horror film. But here we were dealing with the mind of a 13 year old. "Shock Theater" was a relatively recent addition to Detroit's television lineup. Its movie genre centered on the classic horror films of Karloff, Legosi, Price and Chaney. The introduction consisted of the skull and foggy vapor dried ice trick along with the ghoulish raspy voice of some demented bogeyman. Exactly the right mood and setting for my initial foray of nighttime solo funeral home duty. According to the announcer, who no doubt was an authority on the subject, the only cool way to enjoy "Shock Theater" was in the dark. It was past 11 P.M. – I was a brave fearless teenager – I killed the lights. As the feature progressed and the images and their piercing screams and rhetoric echoed throughout the room I found myself moving up in my seat. Then as if on cue the household steam pipes began a symphony of intense clanging and banging. It was about this point in time that this 13 year olds' imagination began to take over the reins of reality. Dead body downstairs – Are all the doors locked? Real or imagined – What was that noise? As the movie and my imagination progressed so did the turning on of lamps and lights. By the time of the eventual arrival of the family, 9074 St. Cyril's illumination rivaled a Briggs Stadium night game. The image got the best of me.

"POPS" Soda Shop was a far cry from "Arnold's Drive-In" of Happy Days fame but its opening in 1956 was greeted enthusiastically by the neighborhood teenagers. It was operated by an older couple who were probably hoping to add to and increase their retirement nest egg. On paper it was an ideal location for this type of enterprise – located on St. Cyril Avenue across the street from Burroughs Junior High School and a few doors south of St. Cyril High School it possessed all the ingredients of an after school hangout complete with soda fountain and jukebox.

It quickly became a magnet for students from both schools and a few with no school affiliation, Greasers and Juvenile Delinquents. Over time it began to attract more "Fonzie" type characters than Richie Cunningham wannabes. In an attempt to protect the social and moral virtues of the St. Cyril coeds, "POPS" was rendered off limits to St. Cyril students by the school administration. This edict was often enforced by periodic visits to that den of inequity by the assistant pastor.

Before the ban was instituted I ventured down St. Cyril Avenue a few times to feed the jukebox a few nickels and partake of a soda or malt. If memory serves me correctly this usually occurred on a Sunday afternoon when I knew the leather jacket crowd attendance would be minimal. I may have been a 90 lb. weakling but I wasn't stupid. Translating it into the vernacular of the day – "I had it made in the shade as I split my pad and with some bread in my pocket I headed for the malt shop to dig some sounds. Hopefully it would be absent of greasers and I could leave without receiving a knuckle sandwich."

Although I do recall an incident involving a representative of the juvenile delinquent brotherhood – I was seated at the counter when Pops delivered a hamburger to one of the juvies a few stools down from me. Taking a bite out of his burger Mr. Tough Guy claimed it wasn't cooked enough and proceeded to fire it back over the head of Pops splattering it against the back wall. My memory fails in regards to the length of time Pops and his wife remained in the dangerous soda shop game. I've often wondered why they didn't move to Florida and open up a less stressful business like a sea shell shop – maybe they did.

I officially became a teenager on March 2, 1956 and joined the ranks of an emerging class of consumers. The business world and corporate America were beginning to take notice of a section of the populace that heretofore was not on their radar – 13-19 year olds. Radio, television and newspaper advertising joined the bandwagon by extolling the latest in teenage fashion, music, fads and entertainment. "You had to have it" became the rallying cry of the day whenever a fashion item or fad's popularity reached a crescendo. Peer pressure was beginning to manifest itself into the adolescent psyche.

I wish that photographic evidence was available today of my "had to have" threads of that era. I'm sure that if a photo did exist it would find its place next to the word "cool" in your Funk and Wagnalls – A pink v-neck sweater over a plain white t-shirt and a pair of black slacks finished off with a pair of black "Flagg Flyer" shoes. "Flagg Flyers" had a metal sliding closure that took the place of laces. For outer wear there was the reversible black and pink zippered jacket. Cool man, cool.

1957 saw the opening of the Mackinac Bridge connecting Michigan's upper and lower peninsula, "American Bandstand" made its television debut, the Russians launched "Sputnik", a gallon of gas was 24 cents, average car price was $2,749 and Detroit was building those cars with taller fins, more lights and more powerful engines. On Detroit's eastside 1.4 miles from 9074 St. Cyril the Packard Motor Car Company produced its last Packard on June 25, 1956 – a black Patrician 4 door sedan. It was an ominous indication of the neighborhood's future.

At about the same time the final Packard was rolling off the assembly line a new "Mystery Car" was rolling off "The World's Largest Assembly Line" one half mile to the north of St. Cyril and Marcus. I refer to it as a mystery car because until now it was a mystery to me. While performing some neighborhood background research for this literary masterpiece I discovered quite by accident the "DUAL-GHIA" Eugene Casaroll was the owner and operator of Automobile Shipping, Inc. one of the first car transport companies in the United States. It eventually became the largest in the industry and worked predominantly for the Chrysler Corporation. During World War II Casaroll formed Dual Motors Company which manufactured special trucks with two engines and generators for the military. In 1954 Chrysler's Dodge Division created a concept car called the "Fire Arrow". The staid and stodgy clouded vision of Dodge executives vetoed production of the "Fire Arrow".

Casaroll was a visionary and purchased the rights to the "Fire Arrow" and modified it for production. He wanted to build a four or five seat sports car. He shipped the frame and drive train to Turin, Italy where the body work and interior was fabricated by the Ghia Coach Builders firm. Once the partially completed vehicle was back in the United States Dual Motors handled the rest - thus its nickname – "The Longest Assembly Line in the World".

Dual Motors and Automobile Shipping, Inc. were located at 9760 Van Dyke just north of Grinnell, approximately one half mile from where I grew up. Over the span of my growing up life, the times I passed by 9760 Van Dyke would have to be registered in the thousands. In addition The Palace BBQ, a local neighborhood hangout of the time period (1956-57) was located right next door to 9760 Van Dyke. Car carriers loaded with new Dodges, Chryslers and Plymouths were visible exiting the complex on almost a daily basis. I never saw a Dual-Ghia. In retrospect various factors were in play in regards to this fact. During their two year limited production, only 117 vehicles made the round trip from Detroit to Turin, Italy. Van Dyke or St. Cyril Avenues wouldn't have been my choice for a test track for a custom made sports car. I'm sure that as one was sold it was bundled onto one of his car carriers and shipped out of town.

Casaroll was also very selective as to who would have the privilege of owning one of his creations. You just couldn't walk in off the street and buy one – you had to be vetted and approved from an extensive waiting list by Eugene Casaroll. I don't remember receiving a Dual- Ghia sales brochure in the St. Cyril mailbox. They were priced at $7,500 back in 1956 ($72,894 in 2021 dollars) and even if Casaroll offered a good neighbor discount I doubt if we would have passed the vetting process. Frank Sinatra, Dean Martin, Desi Arnaz, Richard Nixon were some of the early owners of these custom made autos. There is a story circulating that Ronald Reagan lost his Dual-Ghia to Lyndon Johnson in a high stakes poker game. Find it hard to believe that anyone would play poker with honest Lyndon. Today the Dual-Ghia may be found with other rare and exotic cars on a councours d'elegance somewhere in the world or museum with a price tag of $500,000 and up.

New Dodges were rolling off Hamtramck's Dodge Main assembly line and were being driven night and day down St. Cyril Avenue to Eugene Casaroll's auto hauling complex at Van Dyke and Grinnell. Flatbeds hauling frames to the Plymouth Lynch Road Assembly Plant were banned from St. Cyril Avenue as "No Trucks" signage appeared and they were forced to select an alternate route.

The physical structure comprising the SS. Cyril & Methodius complex featured the church being flanked and connected to on either side by the high school and grade school - the grade school located on the north side of the church and the high school on the south side. In September of 1957 I made the transition from north to south. Entering high school did not alleviate the references to my being the son of a funeral director – there were the occasional harmless taunts of "Mort" or "Digger O'Dell" and the plethora of stale funeral director jokes – "What time did I have to get my date back to the cemetery?" – "Why do they lock the cemetery at night,

people are dying to get in!" and of course my usual comeback –
"Don't worry I'll be the last one to let you down!"

My class doubled in size with the influx of students from
neighboring Catholic grade schools where there wasn't a parish high
school and they chose dear old St. Cyril High as their alma mater.
My original St. Cyril grade school classmates numbered about 30
and most of us had been together since kindergarten. Some seventy
years later a dozen of us still remain friends and in contact.

Basketball and baseball were the only two athletic options
available at St. Cyril High. The venerable old pastor, Fr. Zalibera,was
not a football fan nor an advocate of the gridiron. Basketball was the
dominant sport of the two and the team operated under the moniker
of "The St. Cyril Sharks". The selection of this team nickname
has intrigued me throughout the years as the school was hundreds
of miles from the nearest shark habitat. I have often speculated
that due to the school's proximity to numerous auto plants that
"ENGINES" or "CARBURETORS" or "SPARK PLUGS "would
have been more appropriate monikers. St. Cyril was a member of
the Third Division of the Detroit Metro Catholic High School
League. The Third Division teams included Catholic schools with
the smallest enrollment with a few not even possessing the luxury
of a gymnasium. The gyms featured in the movie "Hoosiers" were
basketball palaces compared to some of the un-heated band box
basketball venues of the Third Division.

"Record Hops" or "Sock Hops" were beginning to make
their appearance at some Detroit high schools in the late 1950's.
Beginning in 1959 St. Cyril's became one of the first schools to
initiate these teen dances in the Detroit area. Father Joseph Nosal,
assistant pastor at the time was the guiding force in this endeavor.
He personally built the complete stereo system from scratch.

Detroit radio disc jockeys along with aspiring local rock and roll bands and singers made occasional personal appearances. Each week saw an increase in attendance and before long crowds of over 500 teenagers converged on the St. Cyril gym floor every Friday night. The recipient of this additional revenue was the athletic department. New basketball uniforms adorned the locker room. Home and away jerseys and shorts, warm up jackets and pants, red and white stirrup socks replaced the aging threads. The St. Cyril Sharks were one of, if not, the best dressed quintets to take the floor in the Catholic League thanks to the likes of Elvis, Little Richard, Dion and the Belmonts, Rickey Nelson, et al and the teenagers of Detroit's east side.

In 1959 we witnessed the introduction of "Barbie" and the microchip, Alaska and Hawaii joined the Union, Buddy Holly, Richie Valens and The Big Bopper bought the ranch in an Iowa cornfield, Nikita Khrushchev couldn't get into the "Magic Kingdom" and I turned "Sweet 16". My thoughts and actions gravitated to the goal of every red blooded American teenager – the driver's license – at least it was in 1959. Many a classroom daydream involved me seated behind the wheel of our second car, a 1957 Ford, cruising the drive-ins of Van Dyke Avenue – Richards, Vet's, Big Boys while sliding the radio's AM dial between "Bobbin with Robin" (WKMH -1310), "Jack the Bellboy"(WJBK-1500) Bud Davies (CKLW-800) or "Frantic Ernie" (WJLB-1400).

The path to licensure began with the Driver's Training Program at Detroit's Pershing High School over on 7 Mile and Ryan. Classroom lectures and instruction bordered on the dull and spiritless, the real action was out on the road course where you put those stripped down '58 Plymouths through their paces. Speeding around at 5 -10 miles per hour you practiced the intricacies of parallel parking, backing up and proper turning etiquette. Upon the successful completion of the course Dad and I drove over to

Connor precinct for the dreaded driver's test with one of Detroit's finest occupying the front seat as you did your thing behind the wheel on the city streets. As luck would have it, as we approached the test area we were greeted by the smiling face of Al, a friend of the family and fellow church member who also happened to be a Detroit Police officer and the driving test guy. He asked me if I was a good driver and I replied in the affirmative. He then issued me my temporary license without the formality of going for a ride. It's not what you know...it's????

This development automatically increased my funeral home duties and responsibilities. Shagging death certificates referred to the journey to retrieve a signed and completed certificate from an attending physician or medical examiner. The death certificate is a vital document relative to the final disposition of human remains. Pertinent personal information will be filled in by the funeral director and the medical portion will be completed and signed by the attending physician or medical examiner. Once fully completed and signed it will be filed by the funeral director with the local registrar of the geographic district where the death occurred - a burial permit or cremation permit will then be issued. By law the attending physician is required to complete and sign the medical portion ascertaining the cause, place and time of death within 48 hours. Sounds simple enough – but alas at times this elementary and uncomplicated process became a bane for the funeral professional.

In ideal situations whenever a death occurred in a hospital or nursing home a death certificate with the medical portion completed would arrive with the deceased. If this did not occur the attending physician must be contacted and arrangements made to sign the certificate. This may entail on the funeral director's part a visit to his office, hospital or at times his residence. There have even been times when doctors made a trip to the funeral home to sign the certificate. One Saturday morning I met a neuro-surgeon at his home in the high rent district and was treated to coffee and donuts. As I mentioned earlier that unfortunately in funeral service there exist individuals who fall beneath the radar, the medical profession possessed their share of radar fallers. Among these were those who I am sure received a failing grade in bedside manner class at medical school. Instances abounded throughout the years whereby for whatever reason doctors refused to sign a death certificate or filled them out incorrectly or incomplete. I even had one mental giant ask me what the deceased died from – I wanted to tell him he stopped breathing. Fortunately these transgressions were not the norm but the timely acquisition of a death certificate was and probably still is a challenging situation that confronts funeral directors to this day.

One of my earlier sojourns was to an East Grand Boulevard nursing home to obtain a signed death certificate. Handing the certificate to the nurse I took a seat in the empty lobby – a seat I occupied for the next hour. I knew the doctor was in as I could hear him conversing on the phone in an adjoining office. Being a "rookie" shagger I sat and endured the wait not wanting to create waves this early in my career. Eventually the egotistical quack signed and I was on my way. I vowed from that day forward that this would never occur again without some type of shagger-doctor confrontation. A lesson learned – my time was valuable too.

Instances abounded throughout the years whereby for whatever reason doctors refused to sign a death certificate or filled them out incorrectly or incomplete. A classic tale that bears repeating involves Jim Alcorn who worked for us and other Detroit area funeral establishments as a freelance funeral director and trade embalmer. Representing a funeral home other than ours Jim traveled to a doctor's office located in a downtown Detroit high rise. Entering the reception area and presenting the certificate to the receptionist he was informed to take a seat and she would have the doctor sign it. After a period of twenty minutes he approached the window to check on the signing progress. She advised him that it would be ready shortly. Another twenty minutes passed and he approached the window and informed her that his time was valuable also and he would appreciate some results. He was given the same response. Within minutes a male figure emerged from the office into the lobby – a figure Jim perceived to be the doctor – his perception was correct. Jim questioned him on his intentions on completing the death certificate. The good doctor expressed his regrets but he was going to lunch and would take care of it on his return. Displaying immense emotional restraint, Jim politely informed him that he had two alternatives – sign it here and now or make a trip to the Wayne County Medical Examiner's office to sign it. Dr. "Arrogance" called Jim's bluff and exited for lunch. Jim proceeded to contact the Medical Examiner, who in turn called the doctor, who in turn left a lobby of patients to drive to the county morgue to sign a death certificate.

Arrogant attitude wasn't restricted to certain members of the medical profession it was also prevalent in certain members of the Medical Examiner's staff. Certain conditions and circumstances required the certification of the death certificate by the Medical Examiner's Office. Parking was always at a premium at the old Wayne County Morgue at Brush and Lafayette which was demolished in 1995. You were often forced to park illegally with the hopes that the local meter maid was at lunch or donut shop. More often than not you were playing "Beat the Clock" – once the certificate was certified you had to navigate to the Department of Health at Herman Kiefer Hospital to file it before its 5 P.M. closure. Certification by the Medical Examiner's office was no more than a five minute process when handled by a competent individual, the problem usually was getting any individual competent or not to wait on you – bureaucratic arrogance was in no short supply. One individual took great pleasure in portraying his self-induced importance by ignoring your presence for an inordinate amount of time. He waited on you in his terms. He also sold real estate on weekends on county time with the added benefit of county phones. Whether he was the target in the following anecdote I can't be sure – I only hope that it was.

The fateful event began with the arrival of a funeral director at the desk of Mr. "I Am Important" to have a death certificate certified - as was his modus-operandi the county bureaucrat ignored his presence. After what he considered to be an excessive period of time to be put on hold the funeral director took action. Whether words were exchanged I'm not certain, but is certain is that the funeral director skirted the desk and planted his fist onto the chin of the unsuspecting employee. He left a hero and became a legend in the Detroit area funeral director's fraternity.

An integral and essential ingredient of any successful funeral home operation was, is and always will be positive, affirmative public relations. First impressions went a long way in maintaining that objective. "Working the front door" (Greeting funeral home visitors) was a significant tool in the molding of a future funeral director - meeting the public, shaking new hands, clasping old ones, projecting an image, selling your self were all part of the front door credo and experience. As a novice in training it was imperative that I attempt to master the act of associating names with faces, especially in the close knit Slovak, church and neighborhood communities in which we operated. The majority of the neighborhood and church membership was aware of my identity- I was Tom Van Kula, the funeral director's son. I had to get to know them. Initially it was somewhat difficult but over time faces and names came together. A trick from the master – Dad, helped me on numerous occasions. If and when I was in doubt as to someone's identity and that I figured would be beneficial for me to permanently retain, I followed them to the register stand and after they signed the register book I would discreetly scan the entry and make a connection. This maneuver worked wonders over the years and prevented some embarrassing moments. Thanks Dad.

I'm not sure of its evolution but it was in full force by the time I was considered mature enough to answer the business phone. On the surface it was considered a positive public relations maneuver, the lending out of folding chairs. It was perceived as a two way street – help the friend or neighbor in their time of need and hopefully they would remember your act of kindness in their time of need. Christenings, showers, birthdays, graduations or just a plain old party were occasions when a call to Walnut 1-4370 could garner you a dozen or two folding chairs for your event. Restrictions did apply: We only had a limited number of chairs to lend out plus a few card tables on a first come first serve basis, had to be returned promptly following the event and had to reside in the neighborhood. The "Chair Book" which contained the lending information was prominently located next to the business phone in the hall alcove in the living quarters. Minor snafus and mix ups occurred throughout the years but overall I would consider it a public relations success – with the exception of one individual.

He and his large family were consummate party givers and it would be safe to say he ranked #1 on the all-time chair borrower list. He was a neighbor, fellow church member and friend of the family. When his wife died he buried her at a neighboring funeral home. Chairs anyone?

One of Dad's earliest calls involved the death of an elderly widower who lived alone - his only surviving relative was a son who resided in California. As the gentleman died at his residence and not under a doctor's care it became a Medical Examiner's case. Numerous unsuccessful attempts were made to contact his son. Eventually Dad connected with the son and informed him of his dad's passing and if he had any requests as to burial arrangements. He crudely replied, "I don't care what you do with the old man, throw him in a trash bag for all I care" and hung up. Despite the request of his son the gentleman was accorded a proper Christian burial.

Joe Mijal was a licensed funeral director who early on in his career assisted Dad on funeral services. Dad supported Joe in his attempt to open his own funeral home through moral support and the lending of supplies and equipment. His funeral home was ideally located next to a catholic church in Hamtramck, Michigan. Unfortunately Joe was divorced and this didn't sit well with the bigoted parish priest – his funeral home did not flourish. But it was his action on Dunn Road that placed him high in the annals of Van Kula Funeral Home folklore.

On this memorable morning Joe was assisting Dad on a funeral service at St. Nicholas Byzantine Catholic Church on Detroit's East Grand Boulevard. At the conclusion of the church services the funeral procession was en route down Dunn Road on its journey to Mt. Olivet Cemetery. Dunn Road ran adjacent to Chrysler's Dodge Main Automobile complex and at its northern terminus lay a multi-track railroad crossing. These tracks serviced Dodge Main and the surrounding manufacturing plants. It is unclear when Joe noticed the approaching locomotive, what is clear was that the freight train was not going to impede the progress of the funeral procession. Throwing caution to the wind and ignoring the flashing red lights, Joe throttled his black Dodge sedan down Dunn Road and came to a screeching halt mid-track. He exited the vehicle and began waving his arms in a frantic gesture to gain the engineer's attention. This was immediately accomplished as brakes were applied and the multi-ton locomotive screeched and squealed to a stop. Content with the success of his mission Joe calmly re-entered the Dodge, sped off toward Mt. Olivet as the funeral procession crossed the tracks. History does not record what transpired in the cab of that locomotive that eventful morning – we can only speculate.

I learned to dress myself at an early age – I learned to dress dead people in my early teens. Clothing was either provided by the family or obtained at the funeral home. Back in the day heading the male wardrobe list of the "old-timers" was the blue serge suit. In most cases it was their first suit purchased in America and was often their only one – they never wore out. Throughout the years it was worn at Sunday Mass, family weddings, christenings, funerals and eventually by the owner at his funeral.

I was often queried if when dressing the body if we cut the clothes. My reply, "Certain conditions precipitated necessary alterations". It was very difficult to present a natural appearance by placing a size 42 suit onto a body frame that had shrunk to a size 36. You did what you had to do. Dad and I worked as a team and over a period of 30 years we buttoned numerous buttons, tied countless ties and zipped a multitude of zippers. People were and still are astonished when I mention the act of dressing a dead body. I'd find it even more astonishing if they accomplished the act without any assistance at all. Dad's standing order throughout the years was, "Whatever they bring in, put on!" Reflecting on an early experience in which he forgot to slip a belt onto a pair of trousers precipitated this edict. This miscue was noticed by the widow and she voiced her displeasure to Dad. He often said if they bring in six belts put them all on. Of course no one ever brought in six belts, but once someone brought in two pairs of shoes. I never told my Dad but I only put one pair on the body – we were a couple of feet short.

Trade embalmers were basically subcontractors who performed their craft on a per call basis for funeral homes in the Metropolitan Detroit area. Throughout the years Dad utilized the services of Lloyd Enos, Emery Metzger, Doug Boucher, Jim Alcorn and Terry Gibney. In addition to embalming they were available as needed to conduct and assist on funerals. On call 24-7 they were a hardy lot- constant exposure to formaldehyde and perpetual physical contact with dead bodies of every conceivable type of death was not a vocation for the faint of heart. Hospitals were required to "Red Tag" bodies that died of a highly infectious or contagious disease. This procedure would serve to alert morgue attendants, pathologists and funeral home personnel to initiate stringent precautionary measures, not only in the handling of the remains but in the embalming process. In rare cases this common sense notification was not always implemented thereby jeopardizing the health of all concerned.

On the other side of the spectrum my brother George often related an incident from his Mortuary School days. He and his fellow classmates were summoned one evening at the behest of their "Old School" embalming instructor to the Mortuary School then located on East Grand Boulevard and St.Aubin. The school was the recent recipient of a traffic fatality and the instructor believed his charges would benefit from witnessing the embalming and restorative art procedure. The definition of restorative art at the time: being the art and science of rebuilding, or reconstructing diseased, mutilated or missing tissue so as to produce normal life-like appearance to the human body. To say the least my brother was doubly impressed: first by the finished product turned out by the instructor and secondly that during the cavity aspiration of the body he held the trocar (a sharp pointed instrument used for withdrawing fluid from the abdominal cavity) with one hand while holding and munching on a cheeseburger in the other. I told you they were a hardy lot.

Flowers were and continue to be an integral component of the funeral service. Some archeologists have found floral samples around ancient burial sites from 60,000 BC. In more recent times their presence was required to mask the odor caused by the decomposition of the human remains. With the advanced modern embalming techniques of today this is no longer necessary. Sending of flowers to bereaved families is to offer sympathy in a meaningful way. The placing of floral arrangements in the chapel was another learning experience I was embarking on. A cardinal rule that you attempted to adhere to was placing the floral arrangements of those closest in relationship to the deceased nearest to the casket. With some very large families this entailed some creative maneuvering of the flower stands. I recall one instance that no matter how many times I rearranged the arrangement of the gentlemen in question he was not satisfied. I gave serious thought to placing it in the casket with the deceased and asking him if this was close enough – but I didn't. I'm reminded of a small sign that Dad had hung in the funeral home office – "We try to do the impossible – Please everybody!"

What goes in must come out – such was the case with the flowers. At times we transferred the family pieces to the church for the services and then to the cemetery. Still in vogue during the 1950's and 1960's was the open flower car. Usually constructed on a Cadillac or Packard frame it resembled a luxury long bed pickup truck. Floral arrangements were placed across the outside bed and under the bed was a casket size compartment for additional flowers or a casket. Flower cars were quite prevalent until Detroit's major cemeteries limited the amount of floral arrangements that they would allow into the cemetery. Dad mentioned that sometime in the 1930's he drove one of the dozens of flower cars in the funeral cortege of a prominent Detroit funeral director as an airplane flew overhead dropping rose petals over the procession.

Whenever the opportunity arose whether it was a Saturday or during summer vacation I began assisting on funerals. Usually the first order of business would be the loading of the flower car and once this was accomplished the flower car would take its position in front of the hearse. The flower car normally led the procession up to a certain point. The flowers had to arrive at the cemetery ahead of the main body (no pun intended) as to allow ample time for their unloading at the grave site. Also individual flowers had to be extracted from the arrangements to pass out to the mourners who in turn would place them on the casket in a final farewell gesture.

It was early on in the "Learning the Ropes" segment of my burgeoning career in funeral service that I was comfortably seated next to the flower car driver as we headed north on Van Dyke Avenue leading a procession to Mt. Olivet Cemetery. A few blocks past Lynch Road he instigated his break from the procession as we began our solo journey to the cemetery. It was not a subtle break – actually it was more of a green light take off at the line at Detroit Dragway. I started scanning the dashboard for the St. Christopher medal. Glancing out the side view mirror I followed the trajectory of floral arrangements sailing off the rear bed and landing on Van Dyke Avenue. The driver took notice also and informed me we didn't have time to stop and retrieve them. I mentioned that this would have been difficult as a DSR bus just ran over them. Arriving at the cemetery and designated grave site we were unloading the remaining flowers that didn't go airborne when Dad and the priest arrived – Dad was not a happy camper as a one sided conversation ensued between Dad and the driver. Unfortunately Dad not only witnessed the flying flowers but so did the immediate family. I never saw that particular gentleman again.

One of Dad's more light-hearted flower car driver narratives took place early on in his career. As was customary procedure, Dad arrived with the priest and altar boys at Mt. Olivet Cemetery before the hearse and funeral procession. After depositing the burial permit into the custody of the cemetery attendant he proceeded to the appropriate gravesite. Upon his arrival six things should have been present: A tent, a freshly dug grave, a burial vault, flowers, an empty flower car and one flower car driver. The last three items were conspicuous by their absence. Leaving the priest and acolytes at the flowerless gravesite Dad drove off in search of the lost sheep. Weaving through the network of cemetery roads he eventually spotted the driver seated on the curb enjoying the last puffs of a cigarette. As Dad approached, the driver appeared quite content with himself as he surveyed the dozens of floral arrangements lining the carpeted pathway to the tent and grave. Dad informed him that unfortunately it was the wrong grave.

The majority of Detroit's funeral homes did not own those shiny Cadillac hearses, limousines or flower cars – they were leased on a per need basis. Scattered throughout the city were livery companies that catered to the funeral homes by providing this service. Each hearse was accompanied by a P.H.D. – Professional Hearse Driver. I consider these gentlemen to be some of the most unrecognized members of funeral service. I can recollect no time during the fifty year existence of The Van Kula Funeral Home that anyone who drove a hearse in our employ was less than professional. They were an integral part of the funeral service: they assisted in the lining up of the funeral procession in all types of Michigan weather, they possessed an intrinsic knowledge of Metropolitan Detroit and suburban churches and cemeteries, plus a comprehensive geographic familiarity of its streets and byways.

Dad's initial choice of livery company was the Dietrich Funeral Car Service located on Hamilton Avenue near West McNichols. In addition to hearses, they provided limousines, flower cars, an ambulance and an ambulance plane. In November of 1953 the owner, Charles H. Dietrich was killed in a plane crash while transporting a body in western Michigan. His wife Helen managed the operation for a number of years until she retired and sold the business.

For many years Dietrich's was the official on field ambulance provider for the Detroit Lions Football team. The red lettered metallic yellow Cadillac ambulance was highly visible parked in the field entrance behind the Briggs Stadium end zone. Dietrich's Sunday ambulance driver was one of Dietrich's daily hearse drivers. Unknown to the 50,000 plus fans and possibly the Lion's themselves was the makeup of the ambulance crew. On more than one occasion funeral directors or sons of funeral directors donned the red jacket and black Dietrich ambulance hat and rode into the game in lieu of a ticket. The Lion's Sunday opponent often dictated the size of the crew. I was never a crew member, but my brother George availed himself of the opportunity to witness a few games. The only drawback to no parking worries and a free sideline ticket was the possibility of an on field injury necessitating a trip to the local hospital via the Dietrich ambulance. When this did occur I've often wondered what the injured player would have thought if he knew he was being carted off the field and into the ambulance by a cadre of funeral directors.

Public Funeral Car Service provided our hearse and limousine requirements once Mrs. Dietrich retired and called it quits. Public was owned and operated by the Murrell brothers- Lester, Carmen, Huston and Bill, all gentlemen in the finest sense of the word and a credit to funeral service. Of the four Bill was my favorite, probably because our sense of humor ran along the same vein. As luck would have it Bill drove the hearse for Public's initial trip for the Van Kula Funeral Home. A hearse trip that throughout the years, much to his chagrin, I would bring to his attention- he drove to the wrong cemetery. Dad and I were positioned at the grave site at Meadowcrest Cemetery awaiting the arrival of the funeral procession. Minutes passed and the procession was not in sight and we both became concerned that something had gone awry. Minutes later, much to our relief, the hearse and cortege wended its way through the gates. An embarrassed and humbled Bill Murrell confessed he led the unsuspecting mourners to Mt. Olivet Cemetery a mile east of Meadowcrest - An honest human mistake that provided fodder for years of good natured ribbing.

The Motor City was the geographic location of the multitude of physical manufacturing plants that produced the automobile and as a result housed its immense labor force - a labor force that was a mixture of white and blue collars. Generally speaking the blue collars normally inhabited the neighborhoods within close proximity to the factory. Depending on your position on the executive ladder usually dictated your distance from the plant – the closer to the top rung increased the travel time to the office. Automobile executives gravitated to the affluent suburbs - on the east side it was the Grosse Pointes and to northern Oakland County it was the neighborhoods of Bloomfield Hills and Birmingham. As far as I can ascertain none resided in the St.Cyril and Marcus area.

When these scions of the auto industry moved on to that big auto plant in the sky the funeral homes that catered to the high rent district attempted to provide an appropriate vehicle for their final conveyance. The Cadillac hearse was undoubtedly and is still to this day the most prevalent chassis in the world of hearses. This posed no problem when the transported was a member of the General Motors family. Back in the day executives of Ford and Chrysler were at a disadvantage as Lincoln and Chrysler hearses were not that prevalent. In a historical footnote, Henry Ford, the founder of the Ford Motor Company died April 7, 1947 and was buried on April 10, 1947 – his last ride was in a Packard hearse.

When someone passed away in their residence it was referred to as a "House Call" – clever minds were ever present in establishing funeral director nomenclature. Dad swung into action the moment of receiving a house call and dispatched himself to the residence as quickly as possible. It could be a half a block away or half way across the City of Detroit, 2 P.M. or 2 A.M., dead of summer or middle of winter. Arriving at the residence and offering his condolences he subtly surveyed the situation to determine his plan of action. Family members, the priest or family doctor may have been present along with representatives of the local police department. The number one objective was to have the remains removed to the funeral home in the most expeditious and reverent manner. At times this was accomplished with little or no difficulty and other instances it manifested itself into a stressful and agonizing period of waiting.

When someone died at home the authorities had to be notified. This initial call was usually to the police who arrived and contacted the medical examiner who in turn contacted the family doctor. If the deceased was under doctor's care and was seen within 72 hours of death, or if the doctor was at the residence and death was by natural causes the medical examiner would release the body to the funeral director. There were times when these requirements were not met and a visit to the home by a representative from the medical examiner's office was warranted who would either release the body or have it transported to the morgue for an autopsy. These visits usually precipitated the stressful and agonizing waiting period. Depending on the time of day, backlog of impending cases and number of medical examiner representatives on call determined their arrival time - a three or four hour wait was not uncommon. Throughout the years Dad and I endured numerous bureaucratic Medical Examiner house call moments.

One of my initial house call experiences occurred at the age of 16 or 17 as I drove Dad to a home located a few blocks from 9074 St. Cyril. We met the deceased's son on the front porch along with two of Detroit's finest. The son informed us that he hadn't had any contact with his dad, who lived alone, for a day or two and upon entering his home discovered that he had died in bed. Standing on the porch it was quite evident that death was in the air as the odor of a decomposing body permeated the atmosphere. Fresh air was at a premium as we entered the home and bedroom where the deceased in an advanced state of decomposition was laying in the bed covered with a heavy blanket and a space heater that was evidently in the on high position alongside. It was at this point in time when one of the police officers bolted from the room through the front door down the steps to the front lawn where he immediately threw up. A short time later as we awaited the arrival of the hearse I was standing next to the patrol car where the officer was occupying the front seat. Casting an inquisitive glance in my direction he asked how we could do this type of work. Without missing a beat I replied I consider this a lot safer than having a gang of hopped up punks chasing me down an alley with a sawed off shotgun. He got my point.

It didn't occur that often but there were times when it was necessary to convert the upstairs living quarters into a funeral chapel. This became obligatory when the downstairs chapel was occupied by one large or two smaller services and additional space was needed for

115

a third call. The initial order of business involved the removal and transfer of all non-essential furniture and household items from the living room and dining room and their transfer to temporary storage in the bedrooms. Remaining furniture was then rearranged in such a manner as to obtain maximum square footage to ensure adequate visitor convenience. Residing two stories below the living quarters was the extra equipment necessary to complete the transformation from residence to viewing room. Folding chairs, drapes, palms, candle holders, kneeler, standing crucifix, register stand, mass-card holder, flower stands, torchiere floor lamps were quietly transported up four flights of 28 stairs to the living room. With the arrival of the casket and deceased the conversion was complete – instant funeral chapel.

One small insignificant problem still remained to be solved – the temporary concealment of the family during the hours of visitation. Family disposition depended on the length of time involved in the requested period of our absence. If it was merely for one evening we normally headed to Grandma's house or took refuge in one of the bedrooms to quietly watch television or complete homework assignments. Durations of an extended nature, one or two days, included extended shopping trips, movies or visits to family acquaintances. At the conclusion of the service which resulted in the temporary disruption of our family life the conversion process was reversed and the household reverted back to a state of normalcy or as normal as things ever transpired in the upper flat over a funeral home. As a youngster when hearing of instances of a parent bringing his work home with him, I was uncertain that whenever a casket replaced the television set in the living room as to whether or not Dad qualified in that time honored custom of the business world.

CHAPTER EIGHT

THE 1960'S

The 1960's have been referred to as the most tumultuous and divisive decade in world history. It definitely was an era of profound change and personal enlightenment in the world of the "Funeral Director's Son". In the spring of 1960 Dad decided to trade in our second car – a 1957 Ford. He drove over to Burke Pontiac on Gratiot near Houston-Whittier to check out the Pontiacs. Lo and behold a few hours later he turned the corner in a 1959 white, 4 door Bonneville Vista Sedan. I was expecting a stripped down Catalina but they made Dad a deal he couldn't refuse – I would be shagging death certificates and delivering flowers to the cemetery in style.

Exiting the hallowed halls of St. Cyril High School in 1961 I embarked on my objective of obtaining a funeral director's license. A journey that I must admit took a little longer than it should have due to various factors- less than stellar study habits, active social life, illness, military obligation – but hey it was the '60's!

The "New Center" area of Detroit was located approximately 3 mile north of downtown in the Woodward Avenue and West Grand Boulevard district. Dominating the neighborhood were two of Detroit's landmarks – The General Motors Building and the Fisher Building. Nestled among them on West Grand Boulevard between

Second and Third Avenues was the Lexington Hotel. Located within the lobby of the hotel was The Lexington Pharmacy.

Charlie, a friend and alumnus of St. Cyril High, was employed at the pharmacy while attending nearby Wayne State University. He informed me that a part time position was available at the store and wondered if I had any interest in becoming a member of the Lexington team. I checked with Dad – I would still be able to continue to assist when needed at the funeral home and the extra income would come in handy. Plus the location of the drug store was convenient – I almost passed it on the way home from class. I informed Charlie to count me in.

I looked upon it as another opportunity to broaden my horizons. The New Center area was a vibrant neighborhood with its commercial and professional entities as well as an abundance of 1920-30 era apartment dwellings. During the day thousands of GM employees filed in and out of their world headquarters a few hundred yards east of the Lexington. Across the street the 30 story Albert Kahn designed Fisher Building contained professional offices and retail establishments. It was also home to the Fisher Theater which began life as a movie and vaudeville house and in 1961 was transformed into a venue for live theater.

During the mid- 1950's whenever it was new model unveiling season my brother George, cousin John Schubeck and myself would spend a Saturday admiring the latest editions to the General Motors lineup that was on display in the lobby of the GM building. We would then traverse the underground tunnel to the Fisher Building and take in a movie at the Fisher Theater.

Ironic that within a few short years into the future cousin John would begin his radio and television broadcasting career on the 21st floor of the Fisher Building at radio station WJR – "The Great Voice of the Great Lakes". A 38 year broadcasting career that eventually took him to news anchor desks in Philadelphia, New York City and Los Angeles. John was one of the few to anchor newscasts on all three network owned and operated television stations in one major market – Los Angeles – CBS, NBC, ABC.

Meanwhile back at the drug store. Arriving on my first day of employment I met the owner – Al Pisa. Al was a laid back type of guy who called everybody "kid". You were on the honor system with Al – there was no time clock. Come Saturday afternoon he'd holler out "Hey kid, how many hours you got"? Duties were varied and included stocking shelves, maintenance, working the counter and making deliveries. Basically I was the go to delivery guy. The mode of transportation was a white Ford Falcon - "Lexington Pharmacy" along with the address and phone number was prominently emblazoned across both car doors.

The Brewster Housing Projects were the largest residential housing project owned by the City of Detroit. It was located on the east side of Detroit near the Chrysler Freeway, St. Antoine and Mack. The complex consisted of six, 15 story apartment buildings. Diana Ross, Mary Wilson and Florence Ballard, (the original Supremes) and Lily Tomlin once called it home. Crime became a major problem in the 1960's and 70's and the projects eventually fell into disrepair – a victim of heroin and drugs. A terminal cancer patient, a patron of the Lexington Pharmacy called it home also. One early evening I was given the keys to the Falcon, the patient's project address and his prescription – codeine. Pulling into the projects with the Falcon signage in full view I might as well have announced my presence with flashing lights, a bull horn and an overhead blimp. My arrival did not go unnoticed among the young men loitering around the apartment complex. Locating the proper building, I parked the car and hustled inside. Entering the elevator

I quickly pushed number 15 – the top floor. Throughout the course of time I've experienced my share of sluggish elevators but none will ever compare with the one I occupied that evening. As it struggled upward it came to a complete stop at the third floor. The doors slowly jerked open and four of the meanest looking dudes entered. I forced a weak smile of recognition- I got the "look" in return. I realized that there was no way in hell that I was going to take this slow boat to China all the way to the 15th floor with these guys on board. The abandon ship alarm began ringing in my subconscious. I reached over and pressed the button for the next floor and exited amid their silent stares and headed for the stairwell. I turned on the afterburners and by leaps and bounds reached the top floor in record time. Rapping on the patient's door, I quickly deposited his medication into his hands, bid him a quick farewell and bolted down the stairs, out the door and into the Falcon. Upon arriving back on West Grand Boulevard I politely informed "Big Al" that I just made my one and only trip to the Brewster Projects, I would make no more. I didn't.

One afternoon as I was in the rear of the store Charlie approached and motioned me to the front of store. Al was waiting on a gentleman and Charlie asked me if I recognized him. Before I had a chance to answer Charlie informed me that it was Gene Chandler, the recording artist who popularized "The Duke of Earl". I was impressed. The Duke was purchasing needles- either he was into knitting or needed to sew a button back on his coat – or not. My horizons were being broadened every day at the Lexington Pharmacy.

Located approximately ¾ of a mile west of Lexington Pharmacy at 2648 West Grand Boulevard were the recording studios and headquarters of Berry Gordy's Motown Records. This was the mid 60's and Motown was hitting its stride in the rock and roll arena.

Concerts under the banner of "Motortown Revue" were being performed by their entire roster of recording artists. Most of the venues of the early concerts were located along the "Chitlin Circuit" in the eastern and southern United States. They eventually travelled the entire United States and were responsible for breaking down segregation barriers in the South. These out of town revues generally lasted for a period of 30 days.

On one of the revue departure days my Lexington Pharmacy delivery skills were called upon to make the trek down West Grand Boulevard to the Motown complex. My cargo – 16 ounce bottles of cough syrup with codeine. Exiting the Falcon I ascended the front porch steps, entered the door to the right and proceeded up a flight of stairs to the second floor. People were floating about in every direction and I was momentarily ignored. I glanced over at the office door bearing the name of Berry Gordy – the office was unlit and unoccupied. He was probably in the basement counting his money. Eventually I was approached by a heavyset Black lady who inquired "May I help you?" In retrospect I should have mentioned that I was there to try out for the Temptations, but I'm sure I blurted out something like – "delivery from Lexington Pharmacy". She motioned to her desk top and said to place it there – no smile, no thank you, no tip. I pranced down the stairs in the direction of the real world and drove the Falcon down West Grand Boulevard towards the Lexington. The Supremes had recently released their hit song – "Where Did Our Love Go?" I thought of reworking the title and submitting it to Berry – "Where Did My Tip Go?" Oh well I could always list "Delivered Drugs to Motown" on my resume.

Thelma (not her real name) was a freelance hair dresser who plied her craft among many of metro Detroit Funeral Homes – ours included. The technical term, coined in 1980, is a desairologist - a specialized caregiver for hair of decedents in a funeral home

121

preparation room. To be honest with you I never heard of the term until now. Thelma was our "Hairdresser". If the deceased had a characteristic hairstyle we would request the family to provide a recent picture to assist Thelma.

During her visits to the funeral home we would often engage in small talk – one of our small talks is worth repeating. In the 1950's Thelma and her husband resided on Gladstone Avenue. One evening as her husband returned home from work at one of the local auto plants Thelma posed a question to him. "Our next door neighbor is starting up a business and would like to know if we'd be interested in investing $500.00?" Her husband was not receptive to the request – "Tell that SOB to get a real job like me, I'm not interested." The next day Thelma informed her neighbor, Berry Gordy Jr. that they would pass on his offer. Throughout her life Thelma found it difficult to lend an ear to the sounds of "Motown".

Resident Training was a one year educational requirement on the academic ladder leading to a mortuary science license in the State of Michigan. It was to be served under the personal supervision and instruction of the holder of a license for the practice of Mortuary Science – I had one of the best – my Dad. One of the requirements was the completion and submission of 25 embalming case reports and every three months an interview with a member of The State Board of Mortuary Science. So every 90 days I drove over to West Grand Boulevard and Warren to The Stinson Funeral Home to meet with Sulee Stinson. In 1960 Sulee became the first black woman appointed to the State Board. A native of South Carolina she exhibited that old world southern charm – she was a neat lady.

I had been performing the majority of the apprenticeship duties and requirements prior to registering with the state with the exception of the embalming process. Witnessing numerous embalming procedures throughout the years I possessed a reasonable knowledge of its procedure. Under the watchful eye of Doug Boucher I was about to embark on my first foray into the ancient art of embalming. There I stood, resplendent in my new pair of gifted rubber gloves and my off white button down surgical gown poised with my scalpel in my right hand – the moment of truth had arrived. Throughout the course of history I'm confident that surgeons and embalmers will attest to the fact that there was something about their "first" incision. Precisely what it was I really didn't know. Perhaps my "something" was in the thought that within the preceding few hours this human being laying in front of me was alive and was someone's marriage partner, parent, grandparent and now their life was at an end. Thoughts of "What am I doing here?" and "Do I really want to do this?" entered my subconscious as I manipulated the scalpel through layers of skin and muscle in an attempt to locate the right common carotid artery and internal jugular vein.

During the one year period of apprenticeship I was schooled in the intricacies of raising arteries, injecting embalming fluid, shaving and bathing a dead body, setting the facial features, various techniques involved in the closing of the eyes and mouth, restorative applications and a vast repertoire of embalming knowledge. My confidence level increased with each subsequent embalming procedure as I completed the 25 state mandated case reports. Resident Training wasn't restricted exclusively to the confines of the embalming room – I assisted Dad in making arrangements, conducting funerals, dressing and casketing bodies and executing the myriad of other details involved in a funeral service.

By virtue of the fact that I was a few credits short of full-time college student status I was graciously assigned a lofty position with the local draft board. Developments were not progressing according to plans in Southeast Asia so LBJ and the Pentagon requested my able bodied assistance. I was a first round draft pick in July of 1966 with a monthly sign in bonus of $87.90 per month. I entertained thoughts of pulling a "George Hamilton" – date one of LBJ's daughters and get a presidential deferment but after checking out their pictures I opted for the draft. And so one bright and very early July morning I arrived at Detroit's Fort Wayne Induction Center and joined hundreds of hung-over conscripts. After Fort Wayne's testing and evaluation process to determine if our medical and mental faculties qualified us to become soldiers we were sworn in as members of The United States Army. Following the nondescript induction we were bussed to the Fort Street Union Train Station – destination Fort Knox, Kentucky. As the train began its 400 mile southern journey I tried to envision what would transpire once we reached our destination. Perhaps a "Welcome to the US Army" catered reception replete with sandwiches and cool liquid refreshments would await us along with a guided tour of the Gold Depository and the Patton Museum. Any thoughts along those lines were quickly dispelled as the bus came to a stop adjacent to a giant "Welcome to the US Army" sign. As the doors of the bus glided open a member of the welcoming committee came on board to extend a personal welcome. In my 23 years I was familiar with a fair share of profanity but this guy elevated anything I might have heard to an astronomical level of obscenity. His expressive diatribe made references to our IQ, physical stature, heritage, girlfriends and our future military career. As we exited the bus other members of the welcoming cadre expressed similar sentiments. Evidently Dale Carnegie's book "How To Win Friends and Influence People" wasn't on the drill instructor's must read list.

After spending ten lovely humid Kentucky days at The Fort Knox Reception Center we were eventually transported to Fort Campbell, Kentucky to begin basic training. Due to the massive military build-up in progress at the time demand far exceeded supply in regards to certain military items. Absent items that generated a favorable verdict in regards to my future deployment were ear plugs – they didn't have any. As a consequence of daily firing of the M-14 rifle I developed a bilateral sensorineural hearing loss with a ringing in my left ear. I was informed by Army medical personnel that the ringing might disappear in weeks, months, years or never. After 55 years we're working on the never. I was given an H-3 on my medical profile along with the following stipulation – "No assignment to any area with habitual gunfire or loud noises". I was not going to Vietnam.

Following eight beautiful sun drenched humid weeks on the Tennessee – Kentucky border of Fort Campbell I headed for the great state of Texas, specifically San Antonio's Fort Sam Houston and The Medical Field Service School- I was going to be a medic. I couldn't figure out the Army's logic – first they trained me to take lives and now they wanted to train me to save them. I made such an impression on the medical school personnel that following the completion of the ten week medic program they assigned me as permanent party. I toiled in the office of Battalion Headquarters, Medical Field Service School four and a half days a week. For some reasons we had Thursday afternoons off – I didn't complain. Due to my exalted position as a battalion headquarters clerk I pulled no extra duty. Fort Sam Houston was referred to as the "Country Club" of the Army and for all I know it still carries that moniker. Bearing that in mind I joined the golf club and enjoyed unlimited golfing privileges for $3.00 per month – War is hell!

It was a lazy, hazy Texas Sunday afternoon as I entered my barracks from a long forgotten outing and was immediately greeted by one of the Black GI's who was laying on his bunk, eyes fixated on the portable black and white TV – "Hey Van, they're burning down your town!" I glanced at the TV and witnessed fires and smoke with the Detroit skyline in the background. I replied, "They certainly are!" It was Sunday, July 23, 1967 and the largest riot and civil disorder of 1967 was in progress. I immediately hustled out to the nearest phone booth (remember them?) and placed a call home. I was greeted by three obnoxious beeps and the recorded voice of the phone lady informing me that "All circuits are busy now. Will you please try your call again later". I probably tried my call later at least 50 or 60 times over the course of the next 48 hours and received the same monotonous message. My family was in a war zone and I was 1500 miles away without any information as to their situation or wellbeing. Newspaper and television coverage was not very specific in identifying specific areas of insurrection – it was either east side or west side.

From the colonel on down, members of the battalion headquarters staff sympathized with my lack of news from home predicament and rendered thankful moral support. Returning from lunch on Tuesday and traversing through the parking lot the solution was right in front of me. I've passed by that particular car every day for the past 8 months and now its attached giant short wave radio antenna alerted me like a beacon in the night. I immediately entered the Preventive Medicine Department across the hall from my office and approached the car's owner, a sergeant whose name I can no longer recollect who was a bona fide short wave radio enthusiast. He was more than willing to help. We perceived that it was only the long distance circuits that prevented me from making a connection with the Motor City. I presented him with a list of local Detroit numbers which he said he would through the magic of radio attempt to contact. Contact them he did. He radioed a short waver in Oakland, California who made contact with a gentleman in Livonia (a Detroit suburb) who placed the calls and obtained information on the status of my family. My parents were in Cleveland, Ohio attending a Slovak Fraternal convention, my youngest brother Jim was visiting his uncle in Southern California, my oldest brother George and his family were living next door to the funeral home and holding down the fort in my parent's absence. When National Guard troops arrived and bivouacked a block away in Lodge Park George decided it was time to get out of Dodge – the family headed to the safety of the in-laws in Bloomfield Hills.

Troop withdrawal began on Friday, July 28 the day of the last major fire - complete troop withdrawal was completed on Saturday, July 29. 9074 St. Cyril and the immediate neighborhood were spared any physical damage from the ravages of the insurrection but psychological forces began to take hold – the white exodus to suburbia immediately accelerated. Ironic that the tools and weapons of war so much a part of Detroit's history in the 1940's would re-emerge two decades later on and in its streets, parks and neighborhoods.

Realizing that the final 9 months of my military career would play out in Texas I decided a change of scenery would be beneficial to my psyche – I transferred myself to Detroit.

Fort Wayne is located in the southwest area of Detroit at the foot of Livernois Avenue in the once proud neighborhood of Delray. Delray at one time was home to a significant number of Hungarians in what was probably the most industrialized area of Detroit. In 1841 Congress appropriated funds to construct a chain of forts from the east coast to the Minnesota Territory, including one in Detroit. During World War II Fort Wayne was the largest motor supply depot in the world. Every single tank, truck, jeep, tire or spare part that was produced in the Detroit factories during World War II that were sent to the battlefronts passed through Fort Wayne. It also housed Italian prisoners of war that were captured during the North African Campaign. It also served as the induction center for the majority of Michigan's men and women entering the Armed Forces.

In the fall of 1967 The Armed Forces Entrance and Examining Station (AFEES) was located within the confines of Fort Wayne. The function of AFEES was to process bodies – I was in my element once again, albeit with live ones this time. In an unpretentious ceremony attended by no one I was appointed Company Clerk of AFEES. In another ironic reflection my office was directly across the hall from the auditorium where I took that fateful step and oath 15 months before. I shared the administrative offices with a colonel, captain, sergeant-major and the female administrator of civilian personnel. I was immediately advised by the sergeant-major that my most crucial and meaningful daily duty and responsibility would be the securing of a pot of coffee from the cafeteria and delivering it to the colonel's office upon his arrival. Eight weeks of basic training, ten weeks of medic training, nine months as a clerk in a battalion headquarters and it all boils down to this – a waiter.

Besides serving coffee I did have additional duties among them was mail clerk. On the first of the month by virtue of this position I became the most popular person on the fort property. AFEES was under the command of Third Army and our monthly paychecks were issued from Fort Sheridan, Illinois and mailed to Fort Wayne. Delivery time at the local post office was sporadic – what else is new? Each morning I would call over to the supply room for my driver and vehicle, head down West Jefferson Avenue to Dearborn Street and the Delray Post Office. Depending on the volume of incoming mail and the mood of the post office personnel dictated the time when we would take possession of the correspondence. Some days there might be two sacks and other times ten sacks or more would await our pickup. The majority of the mail sacks contained records from Lansing or Washington D.C. Various times upon arriving at the post office we were informed that our mail was still in the sorting process. Translation – the slackers in the back were getting paid by the hour.

On those occasions when the mail was not ready for pickup we were confronted with two choices: 1) wait or 2) drive the 1.3 miles back to Fort Wayne and return at a later time. I never chose number 2. It had nothing whatsoever to do with not wanting to return to the office but a simple matter of economics – we were saving the Army money by not making two trips. Delray's Dearborn Avenue presented more enjoyable choices for idle waiting than the confines of the dreary post office building. Locating the nearest establishment containing a pool table we passed the time striking the cue ball and drinking coffee. (It was too early for beer and besides we were on duty). There were no delays on the first of the month – we were on a mission. Our money was in those mail bags. I methodically plodded through those stacks and sack's and extracted the checks under the watchful eyes of post office employees and hustled back to the fort. There was no Dearborn Avenue pool or Delray coffee on the days the eagle pooped.

Fridays were the busiest day of the week at AFEES by virtue of it being Wayne County Day. It is the most populous county in the State of Michigan and Wayne County draft boards scheduled their pre-induction and induction physicals on Friday. It was not your typical Michigan spring day – the sun was out and temperature was above freezing but it was a Friday and Wayne County day. I was seated at my desk more than likely planning my evening social agenda when the phone rang. I let the captain answer it as it gave him something to do and made him feel important. After giving the "AFEES Detroit" greeting to the caller he didn't say much, as a matter of fact I don't believe he said anything at all. He got up from his desk and bolted into the Colonel's office. I could tell by his manner and body language that all was not well in River City – it wasn't. The caller informed him that there was a bomb planted somewhere in the Fort Wayne complex. Unfortunately he wasn't too specific as to its location. The order came down quickly – "Abandon ship" or in Army jargon "Abandon the fort". I grabbed my hat and with keys in hand prepared to beat everyone to the parking lot. Before I could make my move the Captain approached me and told me to head for the cafeteria and clear everyone out and have them line up outside against the West Jefferson fence. I really wanted to get as far away from West Jefferson and Livernois as humanly possible. If he wanted to hang around that was fine with me, after all he was a captain and they always went down with the ship.

I reluctantly headed over to the cafeteria and encountered tables full of potential draftees and recruits scarfing down a free lunch. I jumped on a table and attempted to garner everyone's attention and informed them to get up and get out. The majority heeded my command but a few stragglers were intent on hanging around to finish their meal. I got in their face and informed them that if they didn't get their ass outside and outside quick, this could possibly be their rendition of "The Last Supper". The Medical, Testing and Processing units were evacuated to the West Jefferson fence where records were collected and they were sent home along with all the civilian employees.

Returning to the office the Captain informed me that the bomb squad from Selfridge Air Force Base, located 40 miles away in Harrison Township was en route. In the meantime the Captain issued me another order – "Look for the bomb". Was he nuts? The closest I ever came to a bomb was a cherry bomb back at Lodge Park and I wasn't too crazy about them. Fort Wayne was built in the 1840's and the majority of the buildings were constructed of wood.

In 1967 the structures were a conglomeration of old bricks and old wood. A discarded match would wreak havoc on their structural integrity – no telling what a bomb would do - I wasn't too anxious to find out. I didn't find the bomb, but then again my search wasn't very thorough. The Selfridge Bomb Squad didn't locate it either – they never showed up.

They filed by my desk and into the Colonel's office and closed the door. I quickly surmised that these were not tourists on a guided tour of Fort Wayne culminating with a visit to the commanding officer. They were representatives of Military Intelligence, The Detroit Police Department and The FBI- it was not a social call. They informed the Colonel that Fort Wayne was on the visitor's list of the anti-war protesters. Their objective: To disrupt the orderly operations of the induction center. A plan was formulated to thwart the demonstrator's intentions. Normal operating hours for the AFEES complex were from 8 A.M. to 5 P.M. Testing, medical exams and processing procedures were generally completed by 3:30 P.M. followed by the swearing in ceremony. Troops then boarded busses to be transported to their point of embarkation – train stations or Metro Airport - Their final destination being a military base somewhere in the United States. Generally by 5 P.M. the daily operation was completed.

For "D" day – "Demonstration Day" the timetable was adjusted by two hours – processing began at 6 A.M. with a conclusion goal of 3 P.M. – it worked to perfection. By 3 P.M. the fort was cleared of all recruits, draftees, civilian and military personnel with the exception of yours truly, the Colonel, Captain, Sergeant-Major and a contingent of military police. As the hundreds of protesters arrived from Wayne State University some 6 miles distant they encountered a locked main gate manned in the inside by military police. Their hopes of disruption were quickly extinguished – the busses and troops were long gone. A few speeches highlighted a short rally followed by dispersal back down Livernois Avenue. Final Score – ARMY- 1, HIPPIES- 0.

Prior to the swearing-in ceremony there was an "empty your pockets" ceremony in the auditorium across the hall from my office. The lieutenant informed those assembled that The Armed Forces frowned upon recruits and draftees possessing any personal effects that were not military issued and the list included: pornography, weapons of any type, alcohol, drugs and prophylactics. He further stated that it would be in their best interest to relieve themselves of any of the above mentioned articles at the present time. Two GI's armed with a cardboard box circulated up down and around the auditorium taking up a contraband collection. Prior to my arrival on the scene the final disposition of these items was suspect. Therefore I was saddled with another responsibility – I was appointed property clerk. Every day following the swearing- in activities the contraband box was delivered to me. Questioning the Captain as to what to do with it once it arrived on my desk, he replied "I don't know, find a place for it". A thought crossed my mind but I dismissed it - I was too close to getting out. Scavenging through the bowels of the lower level of our 125 year old building I discovered an empty room. It was perfect – it stank, it was dark and I had the only key. One particular item had a difficult time finding its way to the basement- the latest edition of "Playboy". I figured they wouldn't survive the damp environment so I distributed a monthly copy to each of the officers and some enlisted personnel- I considered it a military morale booster. What was the fate of the stash I left behind when I exited Fort Wayne? I gave the Captain the key. Perhaps the workmen who demolished the building discovered the hidden treasures or do the brass knuckles, switch blade knives and rubbers of the 1960's still exist under the parking lot of today's Fort Wayne?

Another day of playing army was drawing to a close when a young man entered the office. Armed with his draft board notice for his pre induction physical and his medical records he requested to see the Colonel. I escorted him into the Colonel's office and we both took up positions in front of the CO's desk. The gentleman gave his name and requested that the Colonel examine the paperwork of his just completed Fort Wayne physical – specifically the vision portion. Scanning the form the Colonel commented that everything seems to be in order – vision 20-20. "What seems to be your concern?" The gentleman replied, "This" as he popped out his glass eye and deposited it on the Colonel's desk. Once the CO regained his composure he reached for the phone and dialed the Medical Unit. I could sense that the proverbial dung was about to hit the fan so I slithered out of the office and back to the safety of my desk. I didn't want to get involved in any private eye investigation.

July of 1968 was fast approaching and so was the end of my military commitment. While stationed at Fort Sam Houston an integral part of the Medical Field Service School agenda was "The Parade". It seemed that every time a General scratched his butt they threw a parade. In retrospect this made good Army sense. Daily classes left little time for the GI student to play army. The parade was the perfect venue for them to practice marching, close order drill and spit and polish. In my capacity as Headquarters Clerk I planned and coordinated numerous parades involving upwards of 2,500 – 3,000 troops in the Medical Field Service Quadrangle. I wanted a parade!

Due to the complexities of the induction process all required actions did not terminate at the same time. Some individuals finished early and thus became a liability. The swearing-in ceremony wouldn't commence until all registrants were completely processed. Everyone was technically still a civilian until they raised their hand, took the oath and stepped forward. A GI was assigned to monitor and control the early finishers. Weather permitting he might have them outside policing the grounds or just allow them to lounge in the auditorium and await that magic moment. Recreational facilities were non-existent until a ping pong table was ordered in. Unfortunately difficulties ensued transferring it out of the supply room as we ran a multitude of test games to ascertain its quality and dependability. Extreme caution was mandated in regards to the timing of the tests as the supply room was directly under the Colonel's office.

The GI monitor's name is long forgotten but I do recall he had difficulty maintaining rank and that he was from New York City. I approached him one afternoon with my request. He said to be on the porch behind my office in one hour. I arrived at the appointed time – approaching from my left were 100 plus marching "Civilians" led by the "Boy from New York City". It brought a tear to my eye. As they passed me in reviews they rendered an eyes right. I had my parade – the next day I headed for Fort Sheridan, Illinois to become a civilian again.

Returning back to Michigan from Fort Sam Houston in October of 1967 I was forced to live at home as there were no enlisted men's barracks at Fort Wayne. After an absence of 15 months I noticed that times were definitely "a changing" in the old neighborhood. First and foremost was the Chrysler Corporation's addition to the area's skyline – the infamous Huber Avenue Foundry. During my tenure in Texas Chrysler constructed a one million square foot foundry at 6425 Huber Avenue approximately ¼ mile from St. Cyril and Marcus. Ironically it was across the street from my grandparent's former residence of the 1920's. Glowing press releases touted it as the most modern foundry in the world and its air pollution controls among the most sophisticated in the nation.

Unfortunately for the neighborhood pollution control problems surfaced from day one and continued unabated until the facility shut down in 1982.

Neighbors initially began to notice the "foundry dust" as it drifted into their backyards and onto the family wash hanging on their clotheslines. Others became aware of it as they left for work in the morning and found their cars coated with a layer of pollutants laced with fine metallic particles. Sidewalks and front porches were gradually becoming discolored and noxious odors permeated the atmosphere. Numerous incidents occurred when people would enter the funeral home and question Dad and myself as to the origin of the residue on their clothing and their cars. It not only became an embarrassment but a potential disaster for our continuing neighborhood existence as a viable place of business. Calls and complaints to the City of Detroit and The Chrysler Corporation were initially met with scant enthusiasm in their acknowledgement of a problem – a problem that would only intensify with time and eventually signal the demise of my neighborhood.

The story of The Huber Avenue Foundry is a textbook study of corporate apathy and political malfeasance. Chrysler officials, consultants and engineers originally vetoed the concept of constructing a foundry in a residential area – they wanted to build it in Ohio. Enter the City of Detroit and its mayor at the time, Jerome P. Cavanagh. Extracting a substantial equipment tax benefit from the state legislature Cavanagh pressured Chrysler executives to forego "common sense" and their own expert advice and erect the foundry on Huber Avenue – they did. Common sense is a flower that doesn't grow in everyone's garden.

What followed throughout the years of its operation was a litany of pollution control breakdowns, health related issues (neighbors

135

and employees), pitted automobile and home siding finishes, home interior contamination, political and corporate indifference, deception, litigation and a massive decline in the quality of life. The foundry was never issued a permit from the Wayne County Air Pollution Control Commission for their air pollution equipment. I vividly recall many nights witnessing the blowing out of the two roof top foundry cupolas – it reminded me of the annual City of Detroit Fourth of July fireworks extravaganza on the Detroit River.

Except on Huber Avenue this was not a celebration, but a violation. It literally lit up the night sky spewing an assortment of unknown and unhealthy pollutants down on unsuspecting occupants of an eastside Detroit neighborhood. The cupolas were always blown out late at night in the hopes that public detection and angry phone calls would be kept to minimum. It would have been quite a spectacle to have been witnessed by the mayor, city and county pollution flunkies, Chrysler executives and attorneys. But they all resided far away from Huber Avenue – the Mayor five miles distant in his Manoogian Mansion and the Chrysler fat cats and their high priced mouthpieces in the high rent districts of the Grosse Pointes or Bloomfield Hills. I wonder if any of these mental giants ever entertained the thought of erecting the foundry in their pristine neighborhoods. The floating toxic foundry debris would have created quite an uproar as it settled on their swimming pools, luxury cars and manicured estates, not to mention the possibility of it being inhaled by members of the social register. Yuppie protesters would have taken to the streets in their Gucci loafers demanding that Chrysler clean up its act. It never did and never had to – Chrysler Corporation was the largest taxpayer in Wayne County.

Repercussions from July's riot began to manifest themselves throughout the neighborhood. Residential front doors and cars that used to remain unlocked were now being bolted and thrust into the locked position. Homeowners were installing outside security lighting, purchasing guard dogs and contacting real estate agents - Coupled with the Huber Foundry fiasco and a rising crime rate as catalysts neighbors slowly began an exodus to a more civilized environment. Thus began the gradual and methodical dismemberment of my neighborhood thanks to the three "C's" – Chrysler, Crime and Cavanagh. The fourth "C" (Coleman) was waiting in the wings.

In July of 1967 the Eastown Theater the cornerstone of the Harper-Van Dyke neighborhood unplugged its movie projector after a period of 36 years. The Saturday afternoon haven of my youth for cinematic adventure was no more. Adventure of a more sinister form would envelop the structure a few years into the future. It was transformed into a rock concert venue and opened on May 29, 1969 with "SRC" as the headline act. Throughout its existence as a concert venue a multitude of rock and roll heavyweights headlined shows including Seager, Grateful Dead, Nugent, The Who, Alice Cooper, Joe Cocker and The Kinks to name a few. The Eastown's movie theater lobby refreshment center that once offered popcorn, pop and candy was replaced by drug dealers offering LSD, Cocaine, Heroin, Mescaline, Amphetamines and Barbiturates for the pleasure of the concert goers. The Detroit Free Press referred to The Eastown as a veritable drug supermarket and one of the most notorious concert halls in the country. Building violations, non-licensure, rampant drug use, neighborhood pressure and crime all contributed to the demise of the Eastown rock venue after a period of a few years. Thankfully I wasn't into the rock concert scene and the last time I patronized The Eastown they were still showing movies, selling popcorn and Coke as in Cola.

Retiring from my military career several grades below the rank of General I eagerly prepared for the next hurdle in my educational journey – Mortuary School. Yes Virginia there is a Mortuary School. Wayne State University is located inside the city limits of Detroit north of the downtown commercial district. In the 1950's an area of Michigan Avenue, between Washington Boulevard and Sixth Street was laced with bars, liquor stores and pawn shops and was affectionately referred to as "Skid Row". It was home to the homeless and the lower rungs of society. This blight on the downtown district was frowned upon by the Chamber of Commerce and City Hall. Action was taken – they eliminated it. Although the bricks and mortar disappeared the human element survived albeit without a doorway to call home. The majority of the transients migrated one mile north to Cass Avenue which ran north and south and was one block west of Woodward. From two blocks west of Cass (Third Street) and from Temple north to Prentiss Street the area acquired a new moniker – "The Cass Corridor". 627 West Alexandrine was located approximately dead center inside the corridor (pun intended) - 627 housed the Wayne State University School of Mortuary Science.

In the late 1960's Mort School was encircled by low rent tenements, garbage and rodent infested alleys, prostitute flowing dive bars and hourly rate hotels. Anderson's Gardens and The Willis Show Bar two of Detroit's renowned hooker bars of the era were located a block away. Traffic lights weren't the only red lights present in the neighborhood. It was a diverse community of artists, students, professors as well as junkies, pimps and prostitutes. Walls of ivy were absent supplanted by walls of graffiti and paths of meandering grassy knolls of a Midwestern college campus were figments of your imagination.

Memories abound of the derelicts urinating on the front door, propositions from over the hill prostitutes and daily attempts to reach the safety of the building without getting mugged. Broken glass and bottles littered the school parking lot located across the street from 627. The lot was also a source of a continuing battle with local residents who ignored the private lot signage and utilized the terrain as their own. Situations arose where the trespassers' vehicles were blocked in and unable to exit the lot. This did not bode well with the occupants of the adjoining apartment house and in retaliation various acts of vandalism were inflicted on student and staff cars ranging from slashed tires to shot out windows. Detroit police were a constant sight as they filled out and filed numerous incident reports. They then resorted to issuing tickets to the illegal parking perpetrators and an uneasy truce resulted. Whenever possible I took my chances by parking on the street.

The two story building contained classrooms, labs, offices, lunchroom and a library – not unlike a majority of academic structures of higher learning. Adding to its unique educational function it also contained an embalming lab, refrigerated body cooler and dead bodies - The class of thirty included fellow "funeral director's kids" and rookies. Following a brief period of scholastic and social acclimation the class gradually gravitated into two distinct entities- the introverts and the extroverts. We in the second category, which were basically the funeral director kids, affectionately referred to those in the first as "the four pointers". I've always believed that the best offense and defense in the playbook of life for a funeral director's well- being was a sense of humor- it helped to counter balance the pressure and seriousness of a daily dose of death and dying.

Throughout the course of the academic year we were periodically afforded the opportunity to participate in "field trips". In reality they were public relations excursions on the part of various casket and burial vault manufacturers. Trips were local in nature and included a tour of the respective facility and lunch at an above average restaurant. One particular trip as we sat around enjoying post luncheon cocktails we were rudely informed that our presence was requested back at 627 to complete some restorative lab work. Here we sat attired in our finest threads being wined and dined and enjoying the trappings of a corporate expense account when the front office had the audacity to call the game in the sixth inning. Half the class opted to return to the Mort School (guess which half) while the other half including the vault company rep elected to research female anatomy at The Sax Club Go-Go Lounge. Anatomy not being one of my most proficient academic subjects – I chose the Sax Club. If memory serves me correctly the majority of those attending the dance recital were the "the funeral director's kids". The school secretary was less than thrilled with our choice but then again I was never one of her favorites.

Refrigerated storage facilities were located adjacent to the embalming lab and its contents were populated with an anonymous list of Detroit's John and Jane Does. They were embalmed by the mortuary school students under the supervision of a licensed funeral director/instructor. They were always treated with dignity and respect and a local funeral home was contracted by Wayne County for their burial. Periodic visits by the Detroit Police Department were common for the purpose of fingerprinting certain deceased individuals to ascertain positive identification.

Upon my successful completion of Mortuary School and my one year of apprenticeship completed it was time for me to traverse the route to Lansing which Dad navigated in 1933- instead of traveling Grand River Avenue I set sail on the interstate. My destination - The State Board of Examiners in Mortuary Science, my objective- pass the all-day examination to obtain a funeral director's license. Within a short period of time I was notified that I had successfully passed The Michigan State Board Examination as well as The National Board Examination. I was officially licensed as a funeral director in the State of Michigan.

Reflections of "No Tip Berry"!

Historic Fort Wayne Army Post 6325 West Jefferson, Detroit, MI

Delray, Michigan Post Office - 2019
"No more Delray coffee on Delray's desolate Dearborn Avenue"!

Wayne State University - School of Mortuary Science
627 West Alexandrine - Detroit, Michigan
Second Edition

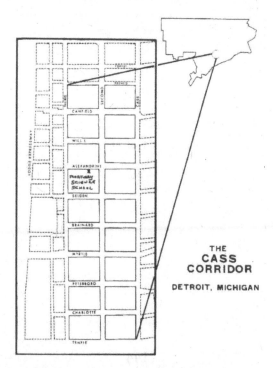

THE
**CASS
CORRIDOR**

DETROIT, MICHIGAN

CHAPTER NINE

THE 1970'S

My Mortuary Science education wasn't restricted to the St. Cyril funeral home or the hallowed halls of the mid-town mort school. Occasions arose down at the local hearse company when additional personnel were required to man the hearses or limousines. Mrs. Dietrich called one afternoon and inquired if I would be interested in driving a limousine for an upcoming funeral at a crosstown funeral home. Not being busy at that particular point in time I answered in the affirmative. Driving over to the Dietrich garage on Hamilton Avenue on the morning of the service I was a little apprehensive. I possessed a certain comfort level working with Dad and our eastside churches and cemeteries – I was heading into unchartered territory. One redeeming factor in driving a limousine that was you followed the hearse to the church and cemetery – all you had to remember was the route back to the funeral home from the cemetery. In the course of time I graduated from limousines to hearses.

Over the next few years whenever circumstances permitted and my services were requested I assisted Dietrich and Public livery companies on a part time basis. This arrangement was beneficial in two ways – 1) the extra income was welcome and 2) I was presented with an opportunity to garner a wealth of funeral service knowledge and experience. I became an active participant in a number of metropolitan Detroit's funeral establishments and became familiar with a variety of diverse churches and cemeteries. By virtue of these sojourns I was also able to tour and observe firsthand the architectural features of various funeral establishments. I was taking notes and looking to the future.

It must be mentioned once again that I was an east-sider and that a fair amount of my hearse trip itineraries occurred west of Woodward and downriver. It was the era of the fold-out map and cellphone GPS was still on the drawing boards. Hanging prominently in the Public Funeral Car garage was a massive map of southeastern Michigan and metropolitan Detroit. Whenever I received a call requesting my services I was given the day, time, funeral home, church and cemetery information. If this happened to be a "first timer" for me I was given more detailed information in regards to location, route of funeral procession to the church and cemetery and this was often repeated and written down upon my arrival at the garage to pick up the hearse.

Arriving at the funeral home I often went over the game plan with the attending funeral director. I can honestly admit that in the beginning of my hearse driving career I experienced a few anxious moments behind the wheel and they all transpired in foreign territory – west of Woodward. There is nothing like the feeling of having 25 cars following you as you approach an intersection when suddenly your written directions fly off the seat onto the floor. It only happened once – after that they never left my sweaty palm. I never missed a church but one time came real close to passing up a cemetery.

In addition to driving the hearse, the lining up of the funeral procession was generally the responsibility of the hearse driver although at some funeral homes you were staff assisted. This particular activity was most enjoyable on blustery snowy Michigan winter days. I was in the process of lining up a funeral procession at a downriver funeral home parking lot when a late model Cadillac Eldorado approached. As it came to a stop I instinctively opened the driver's door for the lone occupant and after ascertaining his position in the cortege he exited the car and entered the funeral home. I entered the Eldorado to move it to its position in the procession and as I slid behind the wheel I quickly slid back out again. I had just sat on a silver plated revolver. My first thought was to enter the funeral home and approach James Bond and inform him he left his gun on the front seat. I'm not a gun guy – I didn't know if this thing was loaded or not – I could have had my rear end configured or worse. I gingerly picked it up and placed it in the side door compartment and moved his car. I eyed him wearily during the afternoon service – I heard of taking a knife to a gunfight – but taking a gun to a funeral?

It was a typical Michigan February morning – cold and devoid of sunshine. It was also a day that didn't play out according to plan. The plan was quite simple: Pick up a hearse at Public Funeral Car Service, pick up a casket at United Casket Company, proceed to The Wayne County Morgue and pick up and deposit deceased in casket, meet Dad and deceased's family at a church cemetery for a committal service. With the downtown Detroit skyline quickly fading in the rear view mirror I headed east on the I-94 freeway on the final leg of the journey to the cemetery.

Traffic was relatively light due to the morning hour as I cruised along in the high speed lane. Without warning the hearse began to decrease in speed – a quick glance at the instrument panel revealed no flashing or warning lights, transmission lever was in the drive position the gas gauge registered ½ tank as we continued to slow down. Glancing over at my brother in the passenger seat we both registered identical looks of apprehension and distress – glancing in the rear view mirror only intensified my feelings. Barreling down on our position and looming larger every second was the front end of a late model Chrysler. I immediately flipped on the emergency flashers, rolled down the windows and we both began frantically waving our arms in an attempt to attract the driver's attention to our predicament. As the powerless hearse coasted to a complete stop so did the Chrysler- within inches of the hearse's rear bumper. Fortunately no chain reactions resulted back down the high speed lane of I-94.

Phase one had passed without any serious physical ramifications although we both shared a case of shattered nerves. Unfortunately two follows one as in phase and now we were faced with an even more demanding test of psychological stress- we were dead in the water. This isn't what I perceived life in the fast lane to be about. Numerous attempts to start the hearse resulted in a negative response. The question that eventually surfaced was "How do you remove one disabled hearse containing two ruffled occupants and one occupied casket from the high speed lane of a major freeway?" As we sat pondering the question amid the abusive stares of passing motorists the answer was quickly forthcoming – approaching six cars behind the motionless hearse was the familiar white sedan of the Detroit Police Freeway Patrol. Talk about being in the wrong place at the right time. Positioning his patrol car directly behind us he radioed for assistance. Within minutes another officer arrived and he proceeded to block all three lanes of the eastbound Edsel Ford freeway as the push bumper of his partner's vehicle gentle nudged the hearse to the safety of the right shoulder.

A conference commenced to plot the ensuing course of action. Priority number one was alerting my Dad of the current situation. Through the magic of police car communications contact was established and a message was forwarded to my mother – "Hearse breakdown – will arrive at cemetery ASAP". My mother called the church and the message was relayed to my Dad and the family. A message I'm sure that did wonders for Dad's blood pressure.

One of the police officers graciously drove me to the hearse company garage where I secured another hearse and drove back to the Edsel Ford freeway joined my brother and the disabled hearse. Now we were confronted with another challenge – the transfer of the casket. I would have to back the good hearse up to the rear of the incapacitated hearse to execute the transfer.

There was not enough shoulder real estate to accomplish a U-turn – I needed help. Leaving my brother and the out of commission hearse for a second time I drove off in search of a phone. I found one nearby on Medbury Street at the Wasik Funeral Home one of the preeminent Polish funeral establishments in Detroit and all around "Good people". It was with some difficulty that I attempted to convince the police dispatcher of my predicament. I'm sure it wasn't too often that they received "freeway body transfer requests". Eventually veracity and tenacity produced results. With the subsequent arrival of the police vehicle the final chapter in our morning adventure was about to commence. With flashing blue lights he pulled out and closed down the eastbound lanes for the second time in less than an hour. I quickly positioned the hearse and with the assistance of the police officer we transferred the casket. He then repeated his freeway stoppage maneuver as we exited the shoulder and proceeded to the cemetery. A subsequent investigation of the out-of-commission hearse determined that the fault lay with a malfunctioning fuel gauge- we ran out of gas.

Occasions often arose when burials took place outside the geographic boundaries of the Detroit Metropolitan area. The mode of transportation was often dictated by several factors: time, distance, location and cost. With the advent of air travel planes gradually replaced the train as the vehicle involved in long distance body transfers. The hearse was utilized for trips that could be completed within a day's drive or less. Dad had the right of first refusal on these out of town journeys and throughout the years he traveled the highways and byways of the Midwest.

One of his more memorable expeditions occurred in the 1960's in Michigan's Upper Peninsula. Among the 25 species of mammals residing in the heavily forested acreage of the UP is the white tailed deer. Driver Glenn and passenger Dad were cruising along the deserted stretch of highway at about 60 MPH and within 20 miles of the destined funeral home when a member of the deer fraternity decided to cross the road (evidently in the corny chicken joke punch line scenario – "to get to the other side."

Leaping from the forested fringes of the roadway the deer in a prime example of poor timing and judgement landed dead center in the cross hairs of the hearse's front end. With the exception of cases of frayed nerves no human injuries were sustained. In those carefree pre-cellphone days a passing motorist contacted the authorities. State Police arrived, the local funeral director arrived with another hearse, the casket was transferred, the damaged hearse was towed and the casketed remains arrived at the funeral home.

One of my initial "out of towners" was a 600 mile round trip to St. Clairsville, Ohio 11 miles from the West Virginia border. Following a local church service the plan was to transport the deceased to a St.Clairsville funeral home for local visitation followed by a next day burial. I pointed the hearse in a southern direction and began my journey. Cruising through the boring Ohio countryside and enjoying the temporary respite from funeral home stress I arrived at my destination in the early evening. Completing the transfer and bidding farewell to my brother funeral director I embarked on the return trip in a contented mood. Dusk was descending on the region as I headed north to the Wolverine State.

Slowly edging past the outer boundaries of some nameless, miniscule Ohio hamlet the evening's silence was shattered by the piercing shrill of a siren. The hearse's rear view mirrors reflected a maze of flashing blue lights. Seeing as I was the only vehicle on this desolate stretch of highway I assumed the sound and light show was in my honor. Adhering to motor vehicle regulations I pulled over onto the shoulder and came to a stop. Additional brilliant illumination bathed me and the hearse courtesy of mega-watt spotlight. Daylight had returned after an absence of only a few hours. I sat and waited. After a period of approximately five minutes my patience level reached its limit. I opened the door and before my feet hit the ground I was greeted with the patrol car loudspeaker command – "Remain in your vehicle". I was back to waiting.

My thought process began to churn out rational and irrational explanations for my sudden detainment. Was I speeding? Negative. Through many travelled miles with Dad and with my own driving experiences one hard core truth emerged – never speed through nameless, miniscule hamlets – especially not in Ohio. Speeding was out. Perhaps there was a prison break or bank robbery and Mr. Policeman imagines this is the getaway hearse or maybe he was just a hard core Ohio State fan who enjoyed stopping vehicles with Michigan licensure. After a few more minutes of vexation footsteps approached the driver's window – the moment of truth had arrived. There he stood in all his glory – a real life "Barney Fife". He was sporting an oversize Smokey the Bear hat and was cradling a very large flashlight. He sported more hardware around his skinny frame than the local ACO. I wondered if he had a solitary bullet tucked away in his uniform pocket? I anxiously awaited his reason for halting my journey. He stated I had no tail lights. After exchanging pleasantries we surmised that the problem would amount to nothing more than a faulty fuse. He informed that I should return to the bustling metropolis that I just passed through as he followed me back to town.

I pulled into the burg's solitary gas station for what I perceived to be a quick pit stop. The young attendant extracted a fuse from the panel and replaced it – six times. A minor fix was transcending into something major. Major problems were diagnosed by the proprietor, a kindly old chap who impressed me as a very conscientious individual – he was. He spent the next 90 minutes checking and rechecking electrical wiring throughout the length of the hearse. He was determined that no vehicle – car or hearse- was going to get the best of him – unfortunately it did. We reached the conclusion that there was indeed a short circuit and its repair was beyond the capability of a small town garage. I was presented a bill for $1.00 – the cost of the fuses. Being the shooter that I was I dumped a ten spot on him and told him to pick up a six pack on the way home.

The continuance of my journey back to Michigan was my next objective. The kindly old mechanic informed me that I was approximately 30 minutes from civilization – well Wooster, Ohio anyway. Flipping on the emergency flashers I headed north hoping Barney wouldn't follow – he didn't. Arriving safely in Wooster and securing a room at the local Ramada Inn the day reached a dramatic conclusion when I was informed that all the area restaurants closed at 10 P.M. It was 10:15 so I headed to the open cocktail lounge, washed down two bags of chips with a couple of Manhattans and called it a day. With emergency flashers flashing I cautiously nursed the hearse back to Michigan in the morning.

THE 1970'S

The highlight of my part time professional hearse driving career transpired on one glorious Michigan Indian Summer Saturday. If truth be known I volunteered for this one. Ethnicity, social, cultural and religious mores are all factors considered in the planning of a funeral. An individual's lifestyle and character are often manifested in their funeral service. A prime example of this premise is exemplified by a "Biker" funeral. A member of a local motorcycle club had a run in with a tree, literally, and was in state at a funeral home on Detroit's East Side. A religious service was to transpire at the funeral home with burial in a suburban cemetery.

As I arrived on the scene I found the attending funeral director in a quasi-state of shock – the events of the past few days were beginning to take their toll. He informed me that during the two day visitation period that there was some vandalism to the building and he was looking forward to a return to normalcy. Perhaps the owners of the neighboring market weren't as anxious for the termination of the funeral as their beer and wine sales spiked considerably within the past 48 hours. This was not your grandma's funeral.

Armed with my car list I exited the funeral home to await the arrival of the mourners. I was immediately greeted by two gentlemen, resplendent in their leathers, sucking on a beer. I instantly perceived that this was going to be a very interesting day – I would not be disappointed. They were heard before they were seen – sporting their colors and club banners they began to approach the funeral home from all directions. When all was said and done over 300 Harleys filled the funeral home parking lot and surrounding side streets. The neighbors turned out en- masse to witness the spectacle. Clutching a handful of funeral flags I stood waiting for the remainder of the immediate family vehicles to arrive when I was approached by a member of the biker fraternity. "Hey man, I need a flag for my bike". To say this dude was spaced out

153

would be an understatement – he definitely had more than a bowl of Cheerios for breakfast. As diplomatically as possible I politely refused his request stating we were only flagging cars and we don't possess 300 flags for the motorcycles – not to mention where would we place a magnetic flag on a Harley? He was insistent and repeated his request – "Hey man, I need a flag for my bike". This conversation was slowly deteriorating - I told him I would go inside and check with the funeral director in regards to his request. I escaped inside the funeral home and exited through another door hoping that Mr. Space Cadet would have disappeared. He did and at the end of the day so did a handful of funeral flags- no doubt memorial souvenirs on display at one or more of the local biker clubhouses.

Although not a member of the biker's inner circle, not even their outer circle, I was nonetheless impressed with their hospitality and sociability. Offerings of beer, wine, whiskey and drags on funny little cigarettes were politely offered and politely refused. Female biker mourning attire was definitely an eye opener – in more ways than one. It was right off the pages of Frederick's of Hollywood catalog. Needless to say it offered a brief respite from the conservative, conventional, drab, black mourning apparel I was accustomed to viewing.

As I continued my parking lot vigil for the remaining family vehicles on the car list a lone female approached. Actually she slithered my way in her skin tight jeans and equally skin hugging halter top. She was grasping a can of ice cold beer – my kind of girl. If she was going to request a flag for her Harley I'm afraid I would have acquiesced. She started to hit on me – at least that's what I'm telling myself some fifty years later. In addition to falling for my charms she basically wanted to ride in the hearse to the cemetery. Okay Mr. Hearse Driver how do you handle this one? I politely informed her that 1. It wasn't my hearse, 2. Company policy forbade any front seat passengers and 3. I've got to get inside as the service is about to begin.

At the conclusion of the religious service the casket was pallbeared to the hearse and mourners filed out of the chapel and retreated to their cars and bikes. Lined up behind the hearse were approximately 24 cars followed by 300 plus Harley Davidson motorcycles. The trip to the cemetery would encompass 23 miles and pass through three Detroit suburbs. Due to the size of the procession and distance involved arrangements were executed for a police escort. Detroit would provide an escort to the city limits wherein the following three municipalities would take over as the procession passed through their jurisdictions. With the roar of 300 Harleys in the background I maneuvered the hearse through the neighborhood escorted by motorcycles of the Detroit Police Department. Exiting Detroit and entering the city limits of Warren, Michigan I began scouring the roadway for phase 2 of the police escort. Approximately ¼ mile north I observed a police car parked on the center median. I gradually slowed down to give him an opportunity to pull in front of me – he didn't. As I passed by I glanced over at the officer behind the wheel reading a newspaper. For all I know he's still there. I was on my own – no more assistance from the Mounties.

I slowed the hearse and procession down as I navigated through the next major intersection alerting drivers in the east and west bound lanes of my presence. It was about this time that six motorcycles left the procession and drove up and surrounded the hearse. The leader of the pack, who I assumed was the leader of the pack pulled alongside my open window. Realizing that we were without any further police assistance he asked me if it would be permissible to take over escort duty. Without any hint of hesitation I gave him a thumb's up. They proceeded to take up positions at the northbound intersections stopping and insuring that all east and westbound traffic was made aware of the presence of the oncoming funeral procession. As I cautiously proceeded through the next intersection one of the escorts had his bike stopped 3 feet in front of an eastbound vehicle his massive arms raised in the stop position – behind the wheel an elderly lady sat mesmerized busy locking her car doors.

Many intersections and startled motorists later the procession arrived without incident at the cemetery. Following a brief religious graveside service those assembled came forward and deposited a shovel of earth into the open grave. It was at this juncture that cases of wine and beer appeared on the scene. Along with the liquid refreshments the smoking lamp was lit and the scent of cannabis circulated throughout the tent. It was time for me to exit. Before I did I would have been remiss if I didn't bid farewell to the funeral director. Being the sympathetic and caring individual that I am, I informed him that the motorcycle club was so impressed with his services that they were going to appoint him their official funeral director. I bid a hasty retreat.

In the early 1970's Detroit's Mayor Roman S. Gribbs and the City of Detroit instituted a series of summer weekend ethnic festivals. They were established with the objective of displaying the rich cultural heritage of Detroit's indigenous ethnic communities. In 1971 the Slovaks were represented in a miniscule presence under the umbrella of "The Captive Nations Festival" – this included the majority of the Eastern European nations still under Communist domination. Although Detroit's Slovak community was not as large as others I believed they deserved their own weekend to shine. It was time to grab the polish – like in wax – not Poland. Fortunately I had a friend in the hallowed halls of city government – Ron Thayer. Ron and I became friends in 1961 at the University of Detroit. Currently he was a member of the Mayor's inner circle of advisors down at city hall. Contacting Ron with questions concerning a potential "Slovak Festival" he informed me that in 1972 the City was going to add four additional weekends to the schedule. I said "I'll take one".

That was the easy part – I had a date and now all I had to do was come up with a festival. I'd just compile a list of Detroit's Slovak churches, lodges, organizations, movers and shakers and send out an invitation for an organizational meeting. Easy?-Right-Wrong! Over 40 invites went out in the mail for the meeting to be held at St. Cyril's social hall -Besides Dad and yours truly only one other gentleman found the time to stop by – not a very auspicious beginning. There were the naysayers who said it couldn't be done – get all the different Slovak groups and churches together on the same page for a common goal. I replied "Did anyone every try?" Perhaps a more personal approach was warranted as I placed numerous phone calls and scheduled another meeting which exhibited a marked increase in attendance. Thus began my ten year involvement with The Detroit Slovak Festival.

Churches and Slovak organizations participated in the three day festival on Detroit's riverfront by providing and selling an assortment of Slovak food, libations, souvenirs and crafts. In addition to local bands and dance groups, we imported entertainment from Canada, New York, Pennsylvania and Ohio. Alex Sandor and his Gypsy band made the trek in from Delray. A Sunday morning a non-denominational religious service was conducted by clergy from Slovak Lutheran and Byzantine Catholic and Roman Catholic churches. Attendance figures for the weekend event averaged in excess of 100,000 people. I surmised that it would be an excellent opportunity for a pre-festival party or dinner-dance and over the course of the next decade banquets were held in the ballrooms of the Sheraton-Cadillac Hotel, the Statler Hotel and the Roostertail. As part of the festivities a "Miss Slovak-Detroit" pageant was held to select a young lady to reign over festival activities. The task of master of ceremonies for the pageant throughout the years was competently handled by Jerry Hodak – Detroit television meteorologist who experienced a 45 year career in broadcasting. Jerry was of Slovak ancestry and a product of the St.Cyril and Marcus neighborhood and attended St. Cyril School until a family move in the ninth grade.

The Stroh Brewery Company was one of the festival sponsors and for many years "Stroh's" was the official beer dispensed throughout the festival grounds to thirsty patrons. In 1972 I received a phone call from John W. Stroh Jr. inviting me to lunch at Detroit's venerable seafood restaurant – Joe Muer's on Gratiot Avenue. Along with board member and good friend John Bucko we joined John W. Jr. and his City Sales Manager, Norm Swanson for a get acquainted meeting and to discuss festival particulars. Over the years John W. became a valued confidant and consultant in regards to festival beer logistics. I enjoyed his expertise and friendship. In 1975 the newly constructed Hart Plaza at the foot of Woodward along the Detroit riverfront became the permanent home to the ethnic festivals. The City of Detroit set an 11 P.M. nightly closing time for the cessation of all festival activities. It was the Saturday night of the 1975 festival when I observed from the festival office trailer that the beer concession of the Slovak Soccer team was still operating past the 11 P.M. curfew. After experiencing a 17 hour day all I desired was a trip home and some much needed sleep. Strolling over to the tent to inform Coach Joe that it was time to close up shop I was met with the harmonious renderings of Slovak folk songs from those assembled. In the midst of those assembled was John W. Stroh Jr. – the soccer players were attempting to teach him the rudiments of Slovak folk singing. John always mentioned that he enjoyed the ethnic festivals more than the country club scene. I mentioned to Coach Joe to turn off the lights and bid everyone "dobru noc" (good night). I have no idea how late the Slovak singing lessons lasted and as long as I didn't receive any negative feedback from the City I didn't care. I do know that the following Sunday morning as I arrived on the Plaza at approximately 8 A.M. fifteen minutes later a Stroh's Beer truck appeared on the scene with a fresh supply of beer and the truck driver guy – my new best friend – John W. Stroh Jr.

In 1976 Detroit was designated as the "Slovak Bicentennial Capitol" for the United States – national events were incorporated within the Slovak Festival weekend. The highlight of the week was the Slovak Bicentennial Banquet held in the grand ballroom of the Hyatt Regency Hotel in Dearborn, Michigan. As part of the evening's program over 800 attendees witnessed a taped address from President Gerald Ford and live remarks from the guest of honor, astronaut Eugene Cernan a Slovak American and the last person to visit the landscape of the moon.

The 1980 Michigan Republican Primary was scheduled for Tuesday, May 20. Detroit's Slovak Festival was to be held on the weekend of May 16-18. Festivals and picnics have always been magnets for crusading office seekers and the 1980 Slovak Festival was no exception.

Governor Ronald Reagan and George H.W. Bush would be in town the weekend of the festival ready to square off in the Tuesday presidential primary. I received phone calls from both camps requesting permission for the two candidates to attend the festival to make their pitch. Among other considerations I perceived it would be good publicity along with the fact that there was a chance for some future White House Slovak recognition – perhaps even an ambassadorship for the Slovak Festival chairman. I informed the Bush camp that we would be honored with George H.W.'s appearance at our opening ceremonies on Friday evening. Governor Reagan would be attending a multi-ethnic rally in Hamtramck on Sunday afternoon and following that event they were requesting a visit to the Slovak Festival. I told them to bring it on.

Various meetings ensued both with the candidate's advance people and the Secret Service. I figured it would be a real human interest moment if I had my two and a half year old son, TJ, introduce Governor Reagan on Sunday afternoon. Via televised political commercials and newspaper photographs we practiced facial recognition – by the time the magic weekend arrived TJ knew who Ronald Reagan was. On Friday May 16, 1980 George H.W. Bush arrived at Hart Plaza accompanied by Governor William Milliken along with a Secret Service detail for the opening ceremonies. Also present was an assortment of Detroit city officials, Festival board of directors, the Slovak Festival Queen and her court and my token Democrat US Congressman, James Blanchard. I asked Wayne County Circuit Court Judge John Hausner to emcee the program. As the strains of the national anthems of the United States and Slovakia drifted skyward Reverend Jozef Mikus offered the invocation. At its conclusion I took my seat between Ambassador Bush and Jim Blanchard with TJ, adorned in his Slovak costume, seated on my lap.

As Judge Hausner began with his introductions TJ glanced up and down the dais and turned to me with a quizzical look on his little face and blurted out, "Hey dad, where's Governor Reagan?" The blurt was overheard by George H.W. Bush as he gave me and TJ a quizzical glance of his own - "Out of the mouth of babes".

Prior to the arrival of the Reagan entourage on Sunday afternoon the Secret Service made their presence known on Hart Plaza. I must give them credit – they were thorough – they even checked TJ's diaper before issuing him his stage clearance pin. Once everyone was seated on the dais TJ and I approached the microphone. Without any hesitation and with a confident air TJ bellowed out "Hello Governor Reagan" much to the delight of Ron and Nancy and the assembled thousands. Detroit's Sarisan Slovak dance ensemble performed a medley of Slovak folk dances and then I introduced the future president. Following his address I presented Nancy Reagan with a Slovak Crystal vase and two dozen roses and Reagan a set of books on Slovak history. I then pinned a "Slovaks for Reagan" campaign button on his lapel and placed two dozen more into the crystal vase. They worked the crowd as they exited the festival and mine and TJ's "fifteen minutes" had come to an end.

One spring morning in the merry, merry month of May sometime in the 1970's I entered the studios of WJBK-TV, Channel 2 laden down with an assortment of Slovak food and pastries. I was to make an appearance on "The Morning Show" with Vic Caputo to plug the upcoming weekend Slovak Festival. Prior to my taking the stage one of my entertainment idols was in front of the camera with the host plugging his weekend appearance at "Friar Tucks" down in Maummee, Ohio. I continue to remind anyone that is interested that back in my television days - Soupy Sales opened for me.

Chairing the Detroit Slovak Festival for ten years was an exhilarating and unequaled experience. It afforded me the opportunity to meet and greet future presidents, governors, a plethora of VIP's and to participate in a series of television and radio appearances. But the most redeeming factor was that the festival provided the moment for the citizens of Detroit and Southeastern Michigan to witness and enjoy the rich and colorful heritage of Slovakia.

Reverend Elemir Jozef Mikus assumed the duties of Pastor of SS. Cyril and Methodius Church in the mid 1970's with the transfer of Reverend Joseph Nosal. Father Mikus fled his native Slovakia to Austria in the 1950's as the Communist regime closed the seminaries of his homeland. He was ordained in Rome in 1957 and arrived in the United States in 1971 and in the ensuing 28 years played a prominent role in Detroit's Slovak Community. During my career in funeral service I was afforded the opportunity to make the acquaintances of and work with an extensive number of Catholic clergy – Father Mikus ranks number one on my list of favorite men of the cloth. His unpretentious and unassuming manner manifested itself in his interactions with all those he came into contact with – to me he was a priest's priest.

The "Prague Spring", a period of President Alexander Dubcek's political liberalization of Czecho-Slovakia began in January of 1968 and ended in August of 1968 with an invasion of 600,000 Russian and Warsaw Pact troops. Tens of thousands of Czechs and Slovaks decided the time was ripe for an escape to the West. Over the next few years over 300,000 freedom -seeking individuals hurdled the Iron Curtain for a better life. A majority of the Slovak emigres journeyed to Vienna, Austria 48 miles west of Bratislava the capital of Slovakia. With most arriving with nothing more than the clothes they were wearing and no place to call home they were in dire need of immediate assistance- enter Reverend Elimer Jozef Mikus.

Recognizing the plight of his fellow Slovaks Father Mikus departed Rome and headed 700 miles northeast to Vienna. With the assistance of Cardinal Konig, the Archbishop of Vienna, he co-founded the "Slovak Caritas" a Catholic relief organization. During the span of the next few years until his departure to the United States in 1971 Father Mikus assisted in the relocation and resettlement of 9,000 of his Slovak compatriots. Utilizing his fluency in six languages to the utmost and along with the resources of "Caritas" he helped relocate emigres to the United States and to the four corners of the world. His devotion to humanity and untiring perseverance did not go unnoticed. In 1972 at Detroit's Slovak Festival Banquet at the Sheraton Cadillac I had the privilege of honoring and presenting him with a "Slovak Freedom Fighter Award." In one of my frequent visits to the St.Cyril rectory he showed me an article that also took notice of his humanitarian efforts. It was from the official newspaper of the Communist Party of the Soviet Union "Pravda" – he was named on a wanted list as an enemy of the state.

Having escaped the oppression of Communist indoctrination in the 1950's he couldn't escape the criminal element prowling the streets of the St. Cyril neighborhood in the 1970's and 80's.

He was held up at gunpoint, two of the German shepherd watch dogs were gunned down and the St. Cyril Church and rectory were targets of numerous break ins. Father Mikus petitioned the Archdiocese of Detroit for permission to relocate and in 1982 property was purchased on Ryan Road in Sterling Heights. The final chapter of the 62 year history of the St.Cyril Avenue church was written in December of 1988 with the celebration of its final Mass. The "New" SS. Cyril and Methodius church was dedicated June 11, 1989. In January of 1999 Father retired to his hometown of Oreske, Slovakia no longer under Soviet domination and on August 6, 2013 he passed away at the age of 86. He was an exalted servant of God, a great patriot of the Slovak people and it was an honor and privilege to have him been a part of my life.

Following Father Mikus to the Motor City was a contingent of Slovak emigres who were quickly adopted by the SS. Cyril & Methodius parish community. Father continued his humanitarian endeavors on behalf of the recent defectors of communism who entered the United States legally. He along with Father Nosal and parish members assisted in securing housing, employment and the necessities of life for families and individuals. A group of approximately 12 young men were billeted in the recently abandoned convent and they immediately began their journey to citizenship. Through the efforts of some parish members the majority were able to obtain employment in the manufacturing sector. One individual was hired as a cab driver which resulted in a short lived career and humorous overtones. Although possessing a very limited English vocabulary and an even less perception of the geography of Detroit he was nonetheless given a taxi cab. Evidently he had no problems in navigating from point A to point B. Unfortunately when picking up a fare he always returned to point A (the location he was familiar with) to begin the trip even though the pickup may have been miles away- he was terminated in two days.

Occasionally it became necessary to hire pallbearers for a funeral service. When this need arose Dad or I contacted Father Mikus who would dispatch six convent dwellers to the funeral home to meet our request. Following church services and burial at Mt. Olivet Cemetery Dad presented each pallbearer with a check. Surprise registered on each of their faces as they were unaware they would be compensated for their time – they assumed they were performing a favor for Father Mikus and the local funeral director. Julius who didn't leave his sense of humor behind the Iron Curtain remarked that if he knew he was being paid he would have cried. In Time Magazine's "Happy Birthday America" issue of July 5, 1976 Julius, his wife Agnes and two boys were included in a feature article "New Immigrants – Still the Promised Land". I accompanied the Time correspondent to their family home and witnessed firsthand the details of their escape from Slovakia. It was an emotional recollection filled with high drama and intrigue.

Absolute secrecy was paramount in any escape attempt from behind the Iron Curtain. For the flight to freedom to be successful it was imperative for the escapee to keep family, friends and neighbors uninformed of any clandestine intentions. The reasoning for the precautions was twofold: 1) If questioned by the secret police they would be innocent of any complicity and 2) they would not be able to provide any facts relating to the escapee's whereabouts or intentions. In addition family members and friends for whatever reason were on record of informing state security personnel of planned escape attempts. And so one morning Julius left his home, wife and two young sons and began his journey to freedom. His plan was to send for Agnes and the boys as soon as he was safely relocated and the pressure from the authorities had diminished.

After clandestinely crossing into Austria he embarked on a path to Vienna, the Slovak Caritas Agency and Father Mikus. He obtained employment as a handyman and groundskeeper on an Austrian estate. He informed his wife of his location and the Slovak State Security police were receptive to her request to visit Julius in Austria with one stipulation – she couldn't take her children.

Months passed and in the interim they secretly formulated a family escape plan. After a period of six months the authorities' interest in Julius' defection was considerably reduced and Agnes and the boys were granted permission for a holiday to Yugoslavia (present day Slovenia). As Tito and the communists still wielded power the Slovak authorities saw no harm in granting permission to visit another commie enclave – after all her husband was in Austria – but not for long. On the prearranged day Julius with his humanitarian employer behind the wheel left for the Yugoslavian border. At a predetermined location Julius exited the vehicle and began an arduous evening ascent of the Karawank Mountain Range of the Southern Limestone Alps. This particular mountain range extends for 75 miles in an east-west direction and is one of the longest in Europe and forms the border between Austria and Slovenia. Meanwhile on the south side of the Alps in Yugoslavia Agnes and her young children sat nervously and apprehensive in a Shell station at the base of the mountain range. She was more than terrified of being apprehended by Yugoslavia's edition of the secret police. The sudden appearance of Julius and a few moments of reconciliation brought momentary relief to her fear factor as they faced their next challenge - the Alps. They slowly and methodically began their ascent north in their final phase on their journey to freedom. Anxious moments developed during their ordeal not the least of which was avoiding detection by elements of the border patrol. Also border residents had a propensity to turn in freedom seekers to frontier guards for a hefty reward. Tense moments arose on a few occasions in the form of barking dogs and in one instance the muffled cries of one of the children that were overridden by the sound of a passing train.

Eventually they crossed over the Austrian border and inhaled the glorious fresh air of freedom. As they descended the Austrian foothills they were greeted by the Good Samaritan in the person of Julius' employer – the estate owner. In the days that followed they arrived at the Slovak Caritas agency in Vienna and Father Elimer Jozef Mikus who assisted them in their journey to the United States – The Promised Land. "Give me your tired, your poor, your huddled masses yearning to breathe free".

In the mid 1970's the twisted criminal minds of Detroit embarked on a new item to steal and fence from unsuspecting law abiding homeowners – leaded glass windows and doors – 9074

St. Cyril Avenue possessed both. At this point in time Dad had moved to a Sterling Heights condo and my brother David was occupying the living quarters of the funeral home. One night a group of sleazebags cut the telephone lines in the rear of the building and then proceeded to remove the two leaded glass entrance doors and two leaded glass French chapel doors. David was asleep in one of the rear bedrooms in the residence and fortunately didn't hear the creeps creeping around. Even if he did he had no means of contacting the authorities with the phones being rendered useless – cell phones were still on the drawing boards. A few weeks after the incident on a Sunday afternoon David left the funeral home unattended for approximately 90 minutes as he drove out to Dad's condo. When he returned so had so had the plundering punks – this time in broad daylight they brazenly removed five leaded glass windows.

The leaded glass capers were reaching epidemic proportions in the Detroit area. So much so that the esteemed award winning columnist of The Detroit News Pete Waldmeir devoted a full column of journalistic prose on the subject. I knew Pete through a mutual friend who was also employed at The News. As a matter of fact it was Pete who introduced me to Manhattans on a few of my visits to some of the watering holes of Detroit's fourth estate. I placed a call to Pete with the hope that he might have some reporter's inside info on the repository of the hot leaded glass disappearing from Detroit's residences. In addition to writing a daily column Pete was hosting a regular segment on the Channel 4 evening news. Informing him of our situation down on St. Cyril Avenue he immediately considered it fodder for one of his television broadcasts. A few mornings later I arrived bearing coffee and donuts and met Pete and his camera crew at the leaded glass bare funeral home. This was not the type of publicity that was needed during the ongoing neighborhood upheaval that was already affecting our bottom line. I agreed to the interview in the hope that it might lead to the recovery of our doors and windows – it didn't.

A few days later I received a call from the detective bureau at Detroit Police headquarters informing me that they had recovered some stolen doors and would I venture downtown to ascertain if they were lifted off the hinges of the funeral home – they weren't. While conversing with the detectives they presented me with a list of antique dealers who they suspected were in the leaded glass fencing racket. Some very prominent establishments were on the list and one in particular is still in business in downtown Detroit. I visited a few, incognito, with the hopes of discovering the contraband but came up empty on my investigative efforts. The whole scenario has soured me on antique dealers and their moral fiber. Due to the extreme number of leaded glass robberies and the encompassing news coverage wouldn't you as a dealer be a tad bit suspicious of a couple of douche bags driving up with a truck or van loaded with leaded glass doors or windows? Wherever they may have ended up I hope their present owners derive as much pleasure as I did in cleaning them – I only hope they use Glass Wax. Who knows someday they may make an appearance on "The Antiques Roadshow".

The St. Cyril and Marcus neighborhood continued its downward spiral along with the rest of the City of Detroit. The so called "White flight" continued unabated into the northern suburbs and beyond. People were literally giving their homes away – better their home than their life. Neighborhood patrols of concerned residents took to the streets – I was an active participant in the one encompassing the St. Cyril area. HUD began to acquire recently vacated houses of the Harper-Van Dyke neighborhood and after a period of time they were abandoned once again and became a haven for the drug dealers and their clientele. Street gangs were replacing the Boy Scout troops – The infamous "Bishop Gang" claimed our neighborhood as its turf. It was being transformed into a full blown ghetto. From its days as "The Arsenal of Democracy" it was being converted to "The Arsenal of Survival".

In the mid 1960's Dad purchased the residence adjacent to the funeral home with the intention of a future expansion project. I sketched out some preliminary plans and Dad and I decided to play the wait and see game before undertaking (pun intended) a major financial enterprise. In the interim Dad rented it out to a recently married couple, friends of my younger sister Audee.

One early evening Audee was visiting next door when a lone male figure bolted from the basement and jettisoned out the back door. I was immediately summoned from the funeral home and a call was placed to the Detroit Police. Unsure of their arrival time due to the extreme volume and the backlog of 911 calls I retrieved the company 45 automatic and headed next door. Unsure if there was more than one perpetrator I entered the basement to investigate. The search was unsuccessful and as I exited I was greeted by two of Detroit's finest who joined me in a second uneventful search of the basement.

A debate then ensued as to the direction the thug might have taken and the possibility of there being an accomplice. As one of the side doors of the funeral home was in close proximity to the rear door from which he escaped it was decided a search of the funeral home was warranted.

Not being familiar with indoor architectural intricacies of 9074 St. Cyril the cops decided I should lead the search. Over time I have pondered the wisdom of that decision and have reached the conclusion that it ranks near the top of the dumbest things I've done in my lifetime. With the funeral director's son as point man we spent the next fifteen minutes exploring the four floors of the funeral home. Leading the group with the 45 firmly gripped in my right hand and the two officers directly behind me armed with shotguns and flashlights we conducted a thorough search of the premises – thankfully we came up empty. To this day I've wondered what if we discovered a scumbag lurking in the shadows – what would have gone down? Whatever would have transpired I believe wouldn't have been in my best interest – I would have been between the cops and the bad guy. I was so pumped up at playing cop that I stopped for a donut on the way home.

It was a delightful Sunday afternoon in mid-October in 1972 and I along with my new bride, Marcia, had just returned to the upstairs living quarters of the funeral home after attending the 12 noon Mass at St.Cyril Church. Mom and Dad were in Boston for the National Funeral Director's convention and we were holding down the fort in their absence. Marcia was in the kitchen putting her culinary skills to the test in preparing lunch and I was in the living room preparing the television for the Lions football game. Before settling down to watch the game I glanced out the front window as I frequently did. I was totally unprepared for the scenario unfolding on Marcus Street. Staggering up the north sidewalk next to the corner market was a skinny female waving and firing a gun at a staggering skinny male on the opposite side of the street next to the St. Cyril Rectory. I immediately called for Marcia to witness the unfolding spectacle as I called 911. Returning to the window I observed "Olive Oil" still popping off shots in "Skinny Dugan's" direction alongside the parish house. Suddenly a Detroit Police squad car approached from westbound St. Cyril and executed a left turn onto Marcus. Exiting with guns drawn and using the car doors as shields they ordered the female to drop the gun- she quickly complied and was handcuffed and placed in the back seat of the cop car. Her male target was likewise cuffed and joined her in the car for the trip to the 15th precinct. They both had trouble walking and appeared to be drunk or stoned or a combination of both. The sudden appearance of the police car led me to believe someone else had placed a call before me or the cops happened to be in the right place at the right time. It was all over in a matter of minutes. Or was it?

As the police car peeled away I hustled across the street to the rectory to ascertain if the priests were aware of what transpired alongside their residence. I was greeted at the front door by a visibly shaken pastor, Reverend Joseph Nosal. He invited me in and led me to the kitchen where the assistant pastor, Reverend Jozef Mikus was seated at the kitchen table. Father Nosal stopped in the doorway leading into the kitchen and pointed to a bullet lodged in the door jamb. The same doorway he was standing in conversing with Father Mikus when the shots rang out on Marcus Street and one of the errant projectiles pierced the kitchen window and lodged in the door jamb. If Father Nosal had been leaning two inches forward the bullet would have entered his head just above his right ear. We retired to his office where he dropped his shaking body into a chair behind his desk. Father Mikus entered with a bottle of Hennessy Five Star to help settle his nerves. We spent the next hour settling nerves and discussing the future of what remained of our neighborhood.

Seven months later another dramatic event occurred on Marcus Street. I was manning the front door during visitation for a pioneer member of St. Cyril church, the uncle of a member of the county judiciary. Being a one car family at the time I was anxiously awaiting the impending arrival of Marcia for the ride home and a late dinner stop. As the highly visible orange VW came into view and turned onto Marcus I exited the funeral home and headed in the same direction. As Marcia exited the car and as I approached a few feet away our greeting was rudely interrupted by the piercing sound of gunfire – gunfire of intimate proximity. Not wishing to become homicide statistics in Detroit's annual bid for the title of "Murder Capital of the World" we made a hasty retreat to the safety of the upstairs residence of the funeral home. After dialing 911 (we should have placed the number on speed dial) and informing them of the block party in progress we hastened to the upstairs back porch to ascertain what the "people of my neighborhood" were up to. Whatever was transpiring at the moment was transpiring rapidly, chaotically and seven houses down from the funeral home – gunfire lit up the evening on both sides of Marcus and the adjoining alley – figures darted between houses, garages and parked cars. Within minutes the entire area was swathed in flashing blue lights of approaching police cars and sirens gradually overpowering the sound of gunfire. The overhead beam from the hovering police helicopter cast an eerie glow over the action below. It was the Universal Studio's Miami Vice Thrill Show in my backyard – then again it might have been a pilot for a new TV show – "Detroit After Dark".

As the dust and smoke and gunfire subsided I hastened downstairs to the chapel to determine if any of the visitors were aware of the outside activity – thankfully they were not. After escorting some people to the safety of their cars in the church parking lot (now a standard procedure) I remained out in front of the funeral home. A police cruiser was stopped at the corner traffic light. I approached the passenger side where the officer sat cradling his gun across his lap and I inquired about the event down Marcus Street. He replied it was an undercover drug bust that didn't go too well. Thankfully they didn't request my services as point man on this one.

It was also around this point in time that a budding entrepreneur entered the neighborhood business community.

Located across Marcus directly north of the funeral was a two family house complete with a two car garage. Over a short period of time the recently moved in occupant of the upper flat managed to fill the garage to capacity with an assortment of merchandise. Merchandise and household items that were separated from their owners during their absence from their residence – clothing, electronics, tools and jewelry were all on display in his makeshift garage thrift shop. The B & E specialist gutted the inside of a blue van and utilized it as his conveyance during his criminal forays throughout Detroit's neighborhoods. Cars and vehicles of all descriptions frequently abutted the street side curb of the funeral home. Some came to buy, others came to sell. As there was no visible signage over the garage word of mouth must have been the means that attracted neighborhood clientele. I wonder if he ever charged sales- tax?

Although the criminal elements and dopers were in close proximity we considered ourselves fortunate that the Van Kula Funeral Home was never a victim of an onsite robbery during visitation hours. A few of the neighboring funeral homes were not so fortunate. Entering the funeral home and posing as visitors the degenerates proceeded at gunpoint to rob the mourners and in some cases removed jewelry from the deceased. Security guards were gradually becoming a part of the landscape at a majority of Detroit funeral establishments.

As the neighborhood exodus continued the volume of funeral services we conducted began a gradual decline. People that left the neighborhood didn't want to return and those few that stayed didn't want to leave. Those refusing to leave were often the elderly who ignored the pleas of their children to get out. They often replied that this was their first house and lifetime residence and nobody or anything was going to force them to move. At times their stubbornness resulted in dire consequences as in the case of an elderly Slovak gentleman who was murdered in a home robbery that netted less than $50.00 in stolen property.

Mt. Olivet Cemetery at 320 acres is the largest cemetery in Detroit and was located 1.7 miles from 9074 St. Cyril and was the beneficiary of the majority of burials of Detroit's vast eastside Catholic community. Mt. Olivet was not immune to Detroit's skyrocketing crime spree of the 1970's and beyond. Cemetery visitors tending to and visiting the graves of their loved ones were becoming victims of carjacking's, muggings and purse snatchings. Increased security also became a part of the cemetery landscape. Mt. Olivet began to experience an increase in dis- interments. People no longer felt safe behind the gates at 6 Mile and Van Dyke and were transferring their deceased loved ones to the suburbs. The majority being re-interred at Resurrection Cemetery 16 miles north in Macomb County. Even the dead could not rest in peace in Detroit.

Since obtaining his license in 1934 Dad maintained a meaningful and friendly rapport with Detroit's funeral directors throughout the years. He was a member of The National Funeral Directors Association, Michigan Funeral Directors Association and was appointed to The State Board of Mortuary Science by Governor George Romney in 1966.

Throughout the course of his career situations arose where his services were desired but were constrained by geographic limitations. The family of the deceased wanted George Van Kula to handle the funeral services but didn't want to travel the distance involved to St. Cyril and Marcus. These were normally families Dad had served throughout the years and had since moved out of the neighborhood to the other side of town or some distant suburb. When these infrequent requests transpired Dad would contact a funeral director in close proximity to the family's new residence and request to rent their facilities - more often than not he was accommodated. After all everyone knew George Van Kula and recognized him as a "standup guy" and a credit to his profession. I can remember only one or two instances when his request was denied.

In the latter few years of our existence on St. Cyril Avenue the family request for a change of venue was more specific in tone and intention – they were afraid to travel to St. Cyril and Marcus. Enter the Wasik Funeral Home – I would be remiss if I didn't take this opportunity to acknowledge the contributions of Jerry and Joe Wasik in the survival of the Van Kula Funeral Home in those arduous years of the mid 1970's. Their unselfish attitude in regards to our plight by providing their facilities for our benefit on numerous occasions warrants a deep felt debt of gratitude.

As the 70's progressed along with the neighborhood deterioration we seriously began to contemplate and explore our future and that of the funeral home. In actuality we were faced with two options – relocate or bail out. We opted to relocate. The majority of Detroit's east siders that were transferring out of the city were choosing the safety of the northern suburbs located in Macomb County. Thus I began my quest in that direction - location, location, location. I flew over various Macomb County municipalities that were all experiencing growth spurts due to the exodus from the Motor City. I took photos and notes which I later combined with my notes and photos from ground level. Thus began a protracted adventure and journey into the world of construction and relocation.

Sterling Heights, Michigan was incorporated in 1968 with a population of approximately 60,000 - in 1978 population figures were approaching 110,000 and it quickly became the fastest growing city in Michigan. Located 16 miles north of downtown Detroit and

12 miles north of St. Cyril and Marcus I began to zero in on Sterling Heights as a potential location for relocation.

Murry Dublin of the Baltimore Sun wrote that "it is a city of subdivisions rather than ethnic neighborhoods." Following numerous discussions, road trips, analysis and investigation Dad and I decided on the southeast corner of Fifteen Mile Road and Schoenherr, Sterling Heights, Michigan as the future site of The Van Kula Funeral Home.

In my investigation I discovered that at the time Macomb County boasted one of the highest concentrations of Catholics in the State of Michigan. No less than 12 Catholic churches were within a 3 to 4 mile radius from the corner of 15 Mile and Schoenherr. It was an ideal location for a family with a Catholic background such as ours. Reflecting on my years of personal involvement in funeral service and reverting back to my hearse driving days and the opportunities it afforded me in viewing other funeral homes, I sketched out some basic plans and ideas – I knew what I wanted.

A friend recommended a friendly architect and we teamed up on the drawing board. Hearing bureaucratic horror stories from a few funeral director acquaintances in regards to time consuming delays in acquiring building permits I formulated a plan. Before submitting a final set of plans for approval, I would meet with the appropriate city departments armed with a basic drawing of the building and get their requirements for the detailed project. Spending an afternoon at the Sterling Heights City Hall I met with representatives of the building and engineering departments and accumulated twelve legal pages of recommendations and guidelines. I met up with the architect and presented him with the paperwork and within a few weeks he furnished a set of plans. I submitted them to the City for approval and within a few weeks instead of receiving a building permit I received the unapproved set of plans. They had more red marks on them than a preschooler's art project – it was like we never met. We followed their recommendations to the letter and were rebuffed. Oh well – back to the drawing boards. More burdensome bureaucratic delays and expense were encountered over the next few months - my favorite was the planning commission meeting. The city was requesting 180 parking spaces and so many feet of greenbelt – there wasn't enough land to meet their request. It was either less parking or more greenbelt – I wanted the parking. We needed a meeting with the wizards of the planning commission to request a variance. As the meeting commenced one of the members was studying the prints I submitted and was confused and stated he couldn't understand the problem or my request – he had the plans upside down. I got my parking. Also adding to the delay was the involvement of three agencies in the granting of an easement on the Red Run Drain which traversed along the rear of the property – none of them processed requests at warp speed. In light of all the bureaucratic maneuvering involved you would have thought I wanted to erect a 25 story office complex with a revolving roof top restaurant instead of a one story 10,000 square foot building on a five acre corner lot.

The mid 1970's was not the most ideal period in history to initiate a construction project – interest rates were skyrocketing and lending institutions were less than enthusiastic in granting loans. Their reluctance was even more evident when dealing with an operation whose bottom line was somewhat stagnant due to the reluctance of people to cross over 8 Mile Road back into Detroit let alone travel to the intimidating neighborhood of St. Cyril and Marcus. I realized we were a few degrees short of a Fortune 500 company but Dad did have a 40 year business track record. At times negotiations with the money people was about as a pleasant experience as a double root canal. After much debate financing was

TOM VAN KULA

obtained, permits were obtained, construction issues were addressed and the relocation project reached fruition. On Sunday, March 19, 1978 The Van Kula Funeral Home opened for business and became the first funeral home in the City of Sterling Heights, Michigan. Thankfully unlike 1934 when Dad experienced a six month wait for his first call the Sterling Heights location registered its first funeral on day one.

178

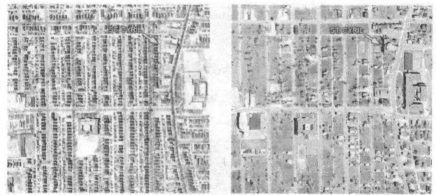

Figure 12a: Detroit Neighborhood Decline Right: 2010 Left: 1950

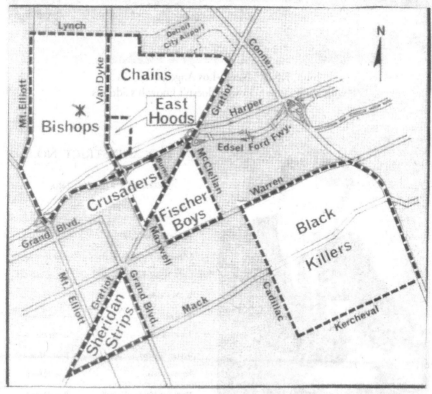

* Van Kula Funeral Home
1975 - Gangs of the East Side of Detroit
We were under the guidance of the "Bishops" "Hail, Hail the GANG'S all here!"

John, KNBC News -Los Angeles -1970's
with his weatherman who doesn't know his address

Cousin John Schubeck
1957 -WJR Radio - Detroit

M. F. D. A. DISTRICT NO. 1

BOARD OF DIRECTORS

1979 - 1980

Thomas J. Van Kula	*President*
Leonard A. Turowski, Jr.	*Vice-President*
Leo J. Miller, Jr.	*Secretary*
William R. Bazan	*Treasurer*
Randall B. Hall	*District Director*
James H. Will	*District Director*
George Stevens	*Board Member*
Boyd L. West	*Board Member*
Mary Kay Hackett Metcalf	*Board Member*

1972
BENDING THE EAR OF DETROIT
MAYOR ROMAN S. GRIBBS -FOUNDER
OF DETROIT RIVERFRONT FESTIVALS

1976-MARCIA,
ASTRONAUT
GENE CERNAN,
TVK AND DAD SLOVAK
BICENTENNIAL BANQUET

1974 SLOVAK FESTIVAL
BANQUET, JERRY
HODAK, DETROIT'S
FAVORITE WEATHEMAN

1976 MICHIGAN GOVERNOR
WILLIAM MILLIKEN,
HELEN MILLIKEN AND TVK

1975 TVK AND
DETROIT MAYOR
COLEMAN YOUNG

TOM VAN KULA, PAULA BLANCHARD, JIM BLANCHARD
JANUARY 1, 1983 1 :00 A.M. LANSING, MI
11 HOURS BEFORE BLANCHARD'S INAGURATION
AS 45TH GOVERNOR OF MICHIGAN

PINNING "SLOVAKS FOR REAGAN" BUTTON ON RONALD REAGAN UNDER THE WATCHFUL EYE OF THE SECRET SERVICE

"FUTURE PRESIDENTS WEEKEND" SLOVAK FESTIVAL MAY 16 - 18, 1980

"TWO GEORGES" H.W. BUSH & VAN KULA

T.J. STILL LOOKING FOR GOVERNOR REAGAN

SS. CYRIL & METHODIUS CHURCH & SCHOOL
9071 SAINT CYRIL AVENUE
DETROIT 13, MICHIGAN

SS. CYRIL & METHODIUS
ERECTED -1926 DEMOLISHED -2003

ST. NICHOLAS BYZANTINE CATHOLIC CHURCH
2384 EAST GRAND BOULEVARD
1921 -1973
VICTIM OF "POLETOWN"

ST. THOMAS
THE APOSTLE CATHOLIC
CHURCH TOWNSEND & MILLER
-DETROIT 1914 -1989

1994
"ANOTHER ONE
BITES THE DUST"

Chrysler Corporation's "Center for Pollution and Neighborhood Disintegration"

Wayne County Morgue - 1956 Demolished December, 1995

Sunday morning on 12th Street July 23, 1967

OPENED OCTOBER 1, 1931

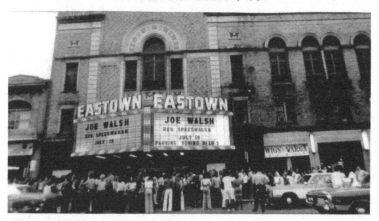

JULY 19, 1973

NOVEMBER, 2015

Van Dyke Avenue just north of Harper -1949

Van Dyke Avenue just north of Harper -2019 What a difference 70 years make!

"Vaporized Neighborhood" Facing south from St. Cyril Avenue and Grinnell

"My Alley" - 2019 Current home for Army Ranger Jungle Training

2019
St. Cyril Avenue

9074 ST. CYRIL AVENUE- 1960'S

2019

GEORGE VAN KULA, SR.; GEORGE VAN KULA, JR.
and THOMAS VAN KULA
proudly invite you to a preview showing
of the First Funeral Home
in the city of Sterling Heights, Michigan
on Sunday, March 19, 1978
from 12:00 o'clock Noon until 8:00 P.M.

VAN KULA FUNERAL HOME, INC.
13650 East Fifteen Mile Road
(corner Schoenherr)
Sterling Heights, Michigan 48077
Phone: 977-7300

CHAPTER TEN

FAST FORWARD

It's not listed on the National Historical Landmarks of Pennsylvania but Dad's residential birthplace of 1903 still exists in the coal patch town of Continental #2 along with approximately 50 other surviving dwellings.

Eighty miles northeast the Village of St. Michael, Pennsylvania the patch town birthplace of my mother Anne in 1911 still contains her childhood home. The St. Michael Miners Museum sits adjacent to the overgrown and abandoned Maryland #1 coal mine.

The J.W. McGinn Funeral Home sign was removed from 92 East Willis Street, Detroit in the late 1940's upon McGinn's death. But the structure built in 1902 where Dad served his apprenticeship in the early 1930's and where he received home cooked cuisine through the basement window still stands.

St. Cyril Avenue once referred to as "The Avenue of Funeral Processions" vacated the title as ethnic churches, their parishioners and funeral homes abandoned Detroit's lower east side on their exodus to the suburbs. The stately Dutch elm trees that once lined the mile long thoroughfare have dwindled down in number to less than a dozen.

The one mile stretch of Van Dyke Avenue from Grinnell Street to Harper Avenue that once was a vibrant commercial entity of my youth now resembles a main street in a Third World country – less than three dozen buildings line the thoroughfare with the majority of those vacant and vandalized.

The once grand and opulent Eastown Theater and in its twilight years a drug infested concert venue was torn down in 2015 boosting the total of Detroit's abundant vacant acreage.

9760 Van Dyke, former address of the Dual Motors Corporation, manufacturers of the prestigious and upscale custom made Dual-Ghia automobiles of 1956 and 1957 still retains a link to automobilia – it's a junk yard.

Packard Motor manufactured its last Detroit car in 1956 at its 3,500,000 square foot complex on East Grand Boulevard – a four door Patrician. The building still stands today although stands may be the wrong word – scavengers and Michigan winters have taken their toll on the storied structure. A structural revival is currently underway in which the current owner's 10-15 year goal is a mixed use development of the site.

After a period of 70 years and the production of 13,943,221 cars Chrysler's Dodge Main Assembly Plant became history in January of 1980. A 1980 Dodge Aspen R/T was the final car to emerge from this historic plant. In 1981 the 67 acre Hamtramck facility was demolished along with its "Poletown" neighborhood of 1500 homes, 144 businesses, 16 churches, 2 schools and 1 hospital. Why – you ask. General Motors wanted to the property to erect a plant to build Cadillacs. GM along with the benevolent assistance of Mayor Coleman Young and the Archdiocese of Detroit utilized eminent domain procedures to displace 4,000 residents from their homes and places of worship and level their neighborhood. It was a close knit community of those of predominately Polish ancestry. Most had lived in those dwellings for 30-40 years or more, raised families, attended neighborhood schools and churches and supported nearby local businesses. In a desperate act of defiance 20 people staged a sit-in at the Immaculate Conception Catholic Church to save it from the wrecking ball. After a period of 29 days a Detroit Police Swat Team invaded the church evicted and arrested 13 people – among them elderly ladies praying the rosary. By midnight of the same day Immaculate Conception Church was reduced to rubble by the wrecking ball – a sterling and defining moment in the history of The General Motors Corporation - and an example of the Golden Rule – "He who has the gold – makes the rules." I'm sure it is safe to say that no GM executives' homes were demolished. In a 1981 Michigan Supreme Court decision by a panel of insensitive justices gave the green light to this act of tyranny. In 2004 the same court reversed its 1981 decision and in a further note of irony in 2018 GM announced the closing of its "Poletown" Assembly plant.

The last Plymouth, a white Grand Fury police patrol car, rolled off the line at the Lynch Road Assembly Plant on April 3, 1981 as Chrysler shuttered its doors and moved the plant's operations to Delaware. As the final 2100 workers became history so did the shot and beer joints lining Mt. Elliott across the street – their function as employee-fueling stations no longer necessary.

Chrysler Corporation permanently locked the gates of its polluting Huber Avenue Foundry in 1986 as its workers pursued asbestos exposure and lung damage litigation. I hope they had better legal representation than the former neighbors. As far as I can ascertain there was an absence of legal permits for the foundry's entire existence. It definitely left its mark on the neighborhood in more ways than one.

The SS. Cyril and Methodius Slovak Catholic Church, Convent, Rectory and School complex was demolished in 2003. The site is now occupied by Flex-N-Gate an auto parts manufacturing plant – part of the I-94 industrial complex that supplanted the vaporized residential area of St. Cyril and Marcus. In 1943 ninety-five (95) Catholic High Schools were located within the City of Detroit with a student enrollment of approximately 64,000 being taught by 1500 members of religious orders – in 2021 three (3) parochial high schools remain within the city limits. One hundred eighteen (118) Catholic churches were located throughout Detroit's neighborhoods in 1943. In 2021 47% of that total remain and of those still functioning as houses of worship most have merged with neighboring parishes and liturgical services have been curtailed. Of the 53% that no longer exist they suffered the fate of demolition, abandonment, vandalism and a place on the Archdiocese of Detroit's burgeoning real-estate docket. A sad and tragic commentary on behalf of those former parishioners who sacrificed "Depression Dollars" to the coffers of the building funds of their respective churches. Today the only remaining remnants of their existence appear in the form of shattered stain glass windows and crushed marble on their desolate neighborhood locations. Century old churches in Europe that suffered the ravages of two world wars still stand – in Detroit they vanish.

St. Nicholas Byzantine Catholic Church relocated from East Grand Boulevard to Detroit's eastside in 1973 and in 2009 left the city and moved to Clinton Township, Michigan. In 1981 the original church building on East Grand Boulevard was demolished as part of the contemptible General Motors "Poletown Project."

John T. Burroughs Junior High School which became Crockett Technical High School which was located across the street from dear old St. Cyril High was closed in 2012 and now sits vacant, vandalized and up for sale – for a mere $125,000 you can take title to this 130,000 square foot relic. Lodge Park (aka Georgia Park) occupies one city block adjacent to the abandoned school – a parcel of land that was once the haven and playground of hundreds of neighborhood residents and the home of "The Lodge Park Panthers". The baseball diamonds have disappeared, the clay tennis courts are fractured, the wading pool is sprouting vegetation, the playground apparatus no longer exist and it remains only as a childhood memory of a vibrant neighborhood of the past.

In 1972 Berry Gordy Jr. took his money and records and high-tailed it out west to Los Angeles. The iconic studios on West Grand Boulevard are now home to The Motown Museum – I returned for a visit once but they didn't remember me.

Wayne State University's School of Mortuary Science located at 627 West Alexandrine in the center of the infamous "Cass Corridor" from 1957 to 2002 moved to Woodward Avenue. This former home of The Springfield Casket Company and subsequent academic institute for future funeral directors and embalmers was converted to a ten unit condominium complex with a hefty mid six-figure and up price tag per unit. I wonder if the tenants were apprised of the building's former tenants. Two of the Mort School's neighbors on Third Street, the Willis Show Bar and Anderson's Gardens were padlocked in 1978 in a prostitution sting. The Willis remained vacant for forty years and resurfaced in 2018 as an upscale cabaret and cocktail lounge. The "Cass Corridor" is experiencing a revival as the dive bars, flop-houses and drug dens of the past decades are being supplanted by upscale shops, trendy bars and restaurants. Property values are increasing with restoration of long neglected residential buildings – it seems the homeless and downtrodden will be on the move once again.

Once the Sterling Heights funeral home became operational the time had arrived to close down and vacate 9074 St. Cyril Avenue. Hiring a truck and a couple of teenage acquaintances I spent a week removing 38 years of furniture, equipment and memories from the house on the southeast corner of St. Cyril and Marcus. The building was purchased by a gentleman who planned on adjusting the interior to apartment rentals. He spent the daylight hours remodeling, unfortunately the neighbors spent the night-time hours un-modeling – whatever he put in they took out. Realizing the futility of the project he abandoned it and within a few short months a fire erupted in the upper floors and not long after my childhood home was demolished. Today the vacant lot remains as a testament to the surrounding vaporization of my neighborhood.

I never had the opportunity to meet Ann-Margret although I did witness one of her performances at Caesars Palace in Las Vegas. Perhaps someday we can get together and reminisce about the idiosyncrasies of living above a funeral home.